THE
IN-HOUSE
DESIGN
HANDBOOK

A RotoVision Book

Published and distributed by RotoVision SA
Route Suisse 9
CH-1295 Mies
Switzerland

RotoVision SA
Sales and Editorial Office
Sheridan House, 114 Western Road
Hove BN3 1DD, UK

Tel: +44 (0)1273 72 72 68
Fax: +44 (0)1273 72 72 69
www.rotovision.com

10 9 8 7 6 5 4 3 2 1

ISBN: 978-2-940361-99-1

Art Director Tony Seddon
Design by Hoop Design

Reprographics in Singapore by ProVision Pte.
Tel: +65 6334 7720
Fax: +65 6334 7721

Printed in China by Midas Printing International Ltd.

THE IN-HOUSE DESIGN HANDBOOK

REAL-WORLD SOLUTIONS FOR GRAPHIC DESIGNERS

CATHY FISHEL

RotoVision

Contents

Selling Your Ideas Up the Ladder

Creative Strategies

03
**In-house Design
in Context**

Working Your Way Up

Preface

"Dad, there's a spider in my room!" That would be my oldest daughter. It's 11 pm and I'm laying in bed reading when she comes in with a tissue and her crippling fear. I get up, go to her room, stand on a chair, and squish the offending eight-legged predatory arachnid. She makes me flush it down the toilet. Twice. She is 19.

My kids squeeze me for everything: time, money, food, cars, cellphones, and they know how to push all the right buttons too. My hair has been falling out from wearing so many hats: father, provider, disciplinarian, ATM, friend, and protector. There are no instruction booklets for parents. No manuals. Just on-the-job training. And it's all tremendously rewarding.

The same goes for in-house creatives. When I'm not killing spiders, I spend my days as a creative director for an in-house design department, which I built from the ground up. And there were no instruction booklets there either. No manuals. Just in-the-house training. I wear many hats there as well: creative director, manager, designer, coordinator, and therapist. But there is one difference, though. After providing creative support for a wide variety of projects over the years, my team and I are beginning to receive recognition for our work and, above all else, Respect (that's right: with a capital R)!

Trends come and go, but there has been a steady growth of in-house creative departments in recent years. In-house design departments like mine are finally starting to get some respect because many companies are now recognizing the benefits of having a strong internal creative team and are leveraging those talents for profit, growth, and success. In-house creatives have complained in the past that they can't get a seat at the table. Well, a few seats just opened up down in front.

Internal creative departments have the potential for being *the* resource for all things design. Design touches every department in a corporation, giving in-house designers a broader range of projects and interactions with a wider range of employees than anyone else in their company. Designers also have access to information and resources that are unavailable to an outside agency, with more opportunities to foster new relationships with colleagues through informal meetings that often take place in the hall or at a coffee station.

In addition, many companies are now providing a boatload of incentives to lure designers to the other side so they can thrive creatively and be happy, productive employees. Regular hours, health benefits, a certain level of security, stock options, onsite conveniences (such as a child development center, health and fitness center, banking, and catering) and more creative workspaces are just a few of the things that have made life on the inside more appealing.

The AIGA, the Design Management Institute (DMI), and other leading trade organizations are realizing that the in-house population is a lot larger than originally believed and are beginning to address in-house issues more than ever. Industry publications such as *HOW*, *Graphic Design:USA*, and *Dynamic Graphics* now feature many articles devoted to in-house design. Design conferences are also including an in-house track and specialized conferences such as the InHOWse Designer Conference are pulling more in-house creatives out of the closet each year.

That's the upside of in-house. On the downside is downsizing, which is impacting a large number of corporate creative departments that don't have the opportunity to grow (that is, add headcount) and who are being squeezed to do more work with less. Outsourcing is also seriously affecting many corporations that have off-loaded service departments to specialized vendors and companies in other countries.

Early in my career as a design manager, I didn't understand how my department fit in with the rest of the organization because back then we had a lack of focus and a weak business strategy. I had to find out what we wanted to be when we grew up. By taking a few steps back, I was able to identify areas where my department could be most effective. Then we implemented processes and workflows that would leverage our strengths and channel our resources to benefit the company's core business groups, which ultimately resulted in financial and service improvements for the company.

But during my in-house tenure I became more and more isolated from the mainstream design culture and was at a loss as to where I could find support for some of the challenges I faced as an in-house design director. Then, in 2002 I was introduced to a creative director who was feeling the same pain that I was feeling. Andy Epstein—then Creative Director at Gund and currently a consultant at Johnson & Johnson—and I spent a lot of time sharing war stories and comparing notes. We found that despite the differences in our companies, we both faced similar challenges. We decided to do something about it and formed InSource (www.in-source.org), an industry trade organization that enhances the understanding, impact, and value of in-house design within the corporate environment. This was an attempt to attract other like-minded people, promote best practices, and build a community. In our early conversations, I realized that the ideas that we tossed around would be of value to other in-house creatives. Again, we did all this by the seat of our pants, with no instruction booklet.

We organized events featuring experts in in-house design management, project management, and brand management, and our membership grew. The isolation that Andy and I felt was prevalent: we found that we weren't alone. Today, InSource continues to provide a forum for the in-house community through our events and our website. And as our organization grows, we've been fortunate to build some solid relationships along the way with designers, publishers, writers, academic institutions, and business leaders.

More recently, I had the opportunity to spread the word at the HOW Conference, the In-HOWse Designer Conference, the Parenting Publications of America Conference, and the Thinking Creatively Conference at Kean University, discussing such topics as how to build and maintain an in-house department, organizational structure, staffing, workflow/project management, keeping your team inspired and motivated, technology and lack of Mac support, rewarding and recognizing good work, charge-backs, promoting your department, playing nice with the agency, department layout, design competitions, onsite convenience, burnout, and, the holy grail, showing the value of design.

And now we have a book on everything in-house. (I wish this book had been around when I was starting out!) This handbook is an invaluable resource for the experienced as well as a primer for the uninitiated. Every corporate creative should have one at their fingertips. Cathy Fishel has organized a comprehensive guide that outlines effective strategies for building, growing, and sustaining a successful in-house creative department. She not only backs it up with theory, but with real-world examples and case studies. So go ahead. Be proud. Working in-house has become a respectable career path.

The phone rings. It's 11:45 pm. "Dad, there's a mouse in my room!" That would be my daughter calling from her dorm at college. Well, gotta go. There are some things you just can't outsource.

Glenn John Arnowitz is Director of Creative Services at Wyeth, a research-based, global pharmaceutical company, where he manages an award-winning team of six designers. He has contributed articles to GD:USA, HOW Magazine, Dynamic Graphics Magazine, *The Creative Group's eZine, and* In-Spired. *His department was featured in the book,* Bringing Graphic Design In-House, *published by Rockport. As co-founder of InSource (www.in-source.org), Glenn is passionately committed to helping in-house creatives achieve design excellence and recognition within their companies and the business community.*

Introduction
What is an in-house designer?

Using the simplest definition, an in-house designer is a professional creative who produces graphic design for, and is an employee of, an organization whose main business is not usually design related.

Using a more jaded definition, an in-house designer is a creative person who finds him- or herself—by choice or circumstance—in an alien world ruled by left-brain-thinkers who undervalue, misunderstand, and in general, do not take full advantage of the benefit design can bring to business.

I say this neither to lull you into this book through empathetic subterfuge nor simply to complain about the unfeeling ways of the corporate world. Both definitions are, in fact, main premises of this book. They are offered here in order to establish our third premise: *any in-house designer who feels undervalued, misunderstood, or in any way ill-treated by an employer needs to take much more responsibility in bettering his lot—that is, prove to the employer, through words and actions that it understands, how design truly benefits business.*

That's what this book is all about. Be ruthlessly proactive. Prove that what you do is valuable. Build on your successes.

As a creative person lodged firmly in a business world, you are a unique character. It can be a lonely post, but you have exactly the same goal as the people who so often disrespect, misunderstand, or step all over your work: you all want the larger organization to succeed.

Chances are, though, no matter how many business magazines publish articles on how accountants or CEOs or warehousing specialists or HR departments can "Learn to be more creative in 10 amazing steps!" you are never going to transform those people into the same kind of creative person that you are. *But you can transform yourself into the kind of businessperson who can very adeptly speak their language.*

2

In this book, we offer many more than "10 amazing steps!" toward that end. You will discover the insights of many in-house design professionals who struggle every day, like you do, to demonstrate to business the extraordinary value of design. We share their successes as well as their failures and hope they teach and inspire you to build a more design-centric organization.

Why work in house?

There are many advantages to working as an in-house designer:

- The in-house designer is usually provided with increased opportunities and benefits as an employee of a larger organization.

- The values of the organization can be inspirational, offering the designer a real sense of community and fulfillment.

- Working for a larger organization provides a sense of prestige and pride, especially if the designer plays a real part in creating the public face of the group.

- As an employee (as opposed to owning your own company), the in-house designer is likely to enjoy more structure, a regular paycheck, and a more predictable schedule. (Many in-house designers report that this is less and less true today however, as companies downsize and try to squeeze more and more work out of fewer and fewer employees.)

- The in-house designer is able to develop a more focused specialization/subject expertise.

- An in-house designer, if utilized properly, is often more cost-effective for the employer.

1 The designer for the ad opposite was given the headline before an image had even been imagined. But when an internal client walked into the design area wearing a retro-style, puffy dress, it inspired the design and the client was eventually photographed in-house for the ad. The combination of her dress, pose, and background created a playful image that was a perfect match for the headline.
Ann Filidoro

2 In-house designers have specialized knowledge that greatly aids their organization. An excellent example is this design for the Metro Day Passes, created by the in-house design team for the Los Angeles County Metropolitan Transportation Authority. Not only do customers keep and collect different color combinations, the passes are also easy for operators to read. The fluorescent inks the designers worked into the palettes also discourage counterfeiting.

1 The undergraduate admissions viewbook for The College of Saint Rose was designed to be cool and slightly alternative to set the college apart from name-brand universities.
Art director, designer, photo-illustrator, writer: Mark Hamilton; designer/photo-illustrator: Chris Parody; writers: Lisa Haley Thomson, Renee Isgro Kelly; project managers: Lisa Haley Thomson, Mary Grondahl; photography: Gary Gold Photography, Paul Castle Photography, Chris Parody, Luigi Benincasa, Benjamin Marvin

■ The constant attention provided by an in-house creative or team benefits the larger organization by building and maintaining a consistent message.

■ The designer has a vested interest in the long-term success of the organization.

■ There is no need to constantly be out beating the bushes for more work, as independent design firms must do to stay afloat.

■ The in-house designer is likely to have more long-term friendships and beneficial business relationships as the result of his or her extended contact with the organization.

■ Unofficial observations indicate that independent design agencies are hiring fewer full-time employees, given the uncertainties of their trade, preferring to work with freelancers instead on a job-to-job basis. The choice of in-house design as a career may offer more stability in the future.

- This last perk is perhaps the most inspirational: through a combination of extended attention to, and superior knowledge of, the organization, *the in-house designer has a better chance to affect real and positive change through design*. As the size or influence of the organization increases, so does the scope of that possible change.

Likely, you may think of other advantages that are specific to your situation. But there is no debating that there are many benefits to working as an in-house designer, to you and the organization. Of course, there are cons as well:

- Even though the organization hired you, it may not perceive that it needs help, change, or even design at all. It may confuse simple production issues with actual design.

- The organization's structure often causes the wheels of change to move very slowly.

- The organization's efficiencies often work against creativity—as in, "Just change the date/color/ headline and run it again."

- The in-house designer can outgrow the challenges of the

organization and become frustrated or burnt out.

- In-house creatives are often pulled in many different directions simultaneously.

- While you wouldn't dream of storming into the accounting department to suggest a new payroll plan or telling the shipping department about how you think they should package goods, it's likely that everyone in your organization has an opinion about design and is happy to share it with you.

- The organization's product, service, or overall philosophy may be dry, conservative, or otherwise challenging creatively.

- While the in-house designer doesn't have to constantly be out in search of new business, he or she does almost constantly have to "sell" ideas to co-workers. And sometimes, of course, the sale is not made.

- Without a company "angel" or champion for design in the form of a supportive CEO or other official, the in-house department lacks respect or attention.

- The in-house designer's bosses may not have training in, or awareness of, creative issues at all. Also, most company's HR procedures, such as employee

2 ChapStick was the official sponsor of TV channel CBS's *Early Morning Show*. This 6 foot (1.82m) tall spinner was used for about a week during the weather segment. The design was created in-house by Wyeth Corporate Graphics to create buzz around the ChapStick brand.
Designer: Cathy Bespalko

2

1 Metro's in-house designers work hard to establish and maintain a friendly relationship with customers of the Los Angeles Metropolitan Transportation Authority. These conversation bubbles are part of that effort: they appear here and there throughout the system to deliver safety and marketing messages. The decals are inexpensive and can be sited and replaced as needed.

2 This postcard for a museum event was designed quickly and inexpensively by the in-house team at the Victoria & Albert Museum. *V&A Design © V&A*

evaluations, aren't built to effectively gauge the performance of an in-house designer, whose output can sometimes be intangible.

- The ongoing training opportunities a company offers or will pay for sometimes don't match up with an in-house designer's needs.

- In-house designers can feel isolated, from others in the organization and from outside creatives.

Again, you are likely to be thinking of your own cons, even as you read. But it's good to know that there are many thousands of in-house creative people in the field today, fighting the same battles as you and even winning a few from time to time.

With more and more corporations around the world awakening to the value of design and creativity, it's a field that's ripe for growth.

1

Friday Late Animate
www.vam.ac.uk/fridaylate

Tim Hale, Fossil, Inc.

It seems fitting to end this introduction and begin the book with an interview with Fossil Creative Director Tim Hale, an in-house designer who began his present career track sitting at a drawing table in the corner of a warehouse. But his story since has been an inspirational one.

1 After 17 years and over 1,000 designs, Fossil self-published a retrospective book celebrating the history, philosophy, and inspiration behind their tin packaging. The book *Tinspiration* was an exciting project for the in-house team. General guidelines were given and a broad team from across the 40-plus design staff were allowed to sign up for and submit ideas for spreads based on tin sets that had been preselected. The project strongly encouraged interaction across established design teams within the studio while providing the net benefit of a well designed, historical, and brand-building artifact for the company that could be used for sales or promotion.

Tim Hale didn't set out to be an in-house designer: in the beginning, he was just helping out a start-up company that made cool watches. But before he knew it, an entire corporation with $2 billion in annual sales grew up around him.

Because he has been at the helm of Fossil, Inc. almost since its very beginning, he has been able to provide the constant leadership that it takes to grow a design-centric organization from the ground up—certainly, an enviable position. Today, he is directly responsible for 75 designers who create everything from print materials and packaging to websites and actual product. Fossil employs more than 200 designers. But remember: he started as a department of one.

Hale also has the benefit of a unique perspective: he was employed by a boutique-type agency prior to coming on board at Fossil in 1987. While he was still at this earlier job, a particular aspect of the in-house groups with whom he worked always puzzled him: their employers didn't seem to take the best advantage of the creative people they hired.

"Why would a company invest in the resource of an in-house design group and not manage that resource better? The work these groups produced was not as good as it could be. That means the company is not challenging them, not managing them, or it hired the wrong people. In my view, there should be little differentiation in quality from what an in-house group or an outside shop would

1

1 & **2** Design not directly related to product/service sales is rare. But design with such remarkable creativity, that articulates the brand value and has entertainment value is a very important branding vehicle for Fossil. These signed and numbered, limited-edition silkscreen posters (two in a set of four) are sold through Fossil's catalog and retail stores.
Design and art direction: Greg Wolverton.

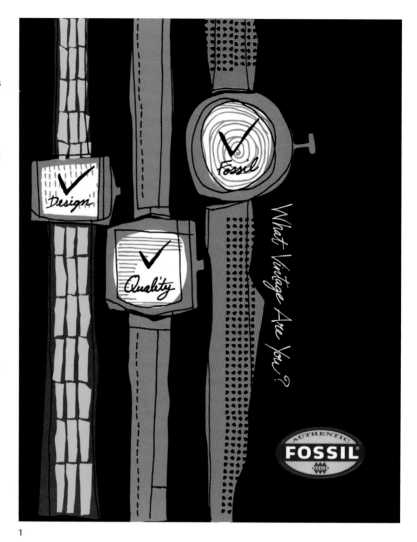

1

produce. When I came to Fossil, my agenda was to prove this model," he says.

In-house design groups, he knows, are sometimes regarded disparagingly by outside groups and—sadly—even by their employers' management. But Hale believes there is sometimes just

cause: those in-house groups simply have not proven the value of their work. Designers working inside of an organization have an even greater responsibility to show the power of design and how it can benefit business: in the twenty-first century, it seems like the entire business culture has jumped onto a creative jet stream.

"There has always been an undercurrent of businesses who have used creativity and who have had great success—Target, Starbucks, and so on. But it is now just bubbling to the surface for everyone else. *Fast Company*, *Business Week*, and other publications are giving a lot more lip service to design as a profession as well as a design catalyst," Hale says. "Now, success is geared around how creative people can be with what is already out there and available to everyone else—information, technology, and such. Companies who have an in-house design group have a real advantage over those who don't."

Hale acknowledges that in-house designers are often not given the opportunity by their employers to make that kind of difference. Because of this lack of regard, he believes in-house creatives must adopt a more proactive stance and become much more analytical in how they approach management. Over time, he says, designers can establish more of a partnership, as opposed to a "helper" model. It's the difference between a company having design in its DNA or just having a quick coat of paint.

The desired partnership is also a moving target, he notes, making it even harder to achieve. When he started with Fossil, his drawing table and all of his supplies were literally tucked into the corner of

"Companies who have an in-house design group have a real advantage over those who don't."

the company's warehouse. Fossil has grown from being a very small, privately owned company to an enormous, publicly traded company: nothing is the same as it was when he started. But one philosophy has continued to drive his success.

"As your company grows and changes, just to preserve yourself, you can't personalize everything that comes to you. It's too debilitating. You have to remove yourself from the comments and actions of others, and begin to understand what is driving these business decisions, whether you like them or not. That's how you learn to make the kind of decisions that make design work in your company."

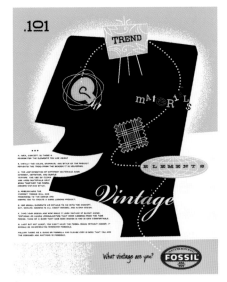

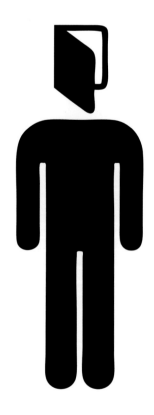

1

In-House Design in Theory

Defining Your Position

For what felt like the 100th time in the same month, Tristan was sitting in a meeting where he felt about as useful as the horrible landscape scenes that were hanging in cheap frames on the conference room's walls. His department manager insisted that he attend these planning meetings so he could "hear what was going on." But no one ever asked his opinion or indeed even inquired what the design department might be able to offer. He got to hear "what was going on" with their budget, their calendar, and every project the design department would eventually be asked to do. But ask his opinion on anything? Never.

Tristan had begun to think of the worst of the framed prints—a particularly trite and sun-faded reproduction of mallard ducks descending on a pond—as symbolic of this entire company. No aesthetic, no imagination. The conference room had "art" because that's what conference rooms were supposed to have. His employer had an in-house designer because their competitors had designers. The company had tri-fold brochures because that's what companies were supposed to have—although he'd told them again and again that redesigning their website would generate more sales. And the brochures weren't even that great looking: by the time all of the departments had had a whack at his designs, they were so

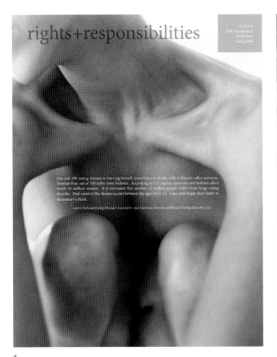

1

2

crammed full of type that no amount of design attention could help. He felt like nothing more than a pair of hands. He felt powerless.

Sound familiar? Likely, it does, at least in part. What in-house designer hasn't had that incredible sinking feeling when he sees yet another episode of "design by committee" beginning? Who hasn't had their budget or schedule slashed? Who hasn't felt that lack of respect or understanding?

But just as familiar is that wonderful sensation of success, when you know that the work you did will make a real difference for your organization, that your creativity will move your employer forward in some way, however incremental. You can envision that success. You can see how design can benefit the larger group.

So why can't your employer or co-workers see it just as clearly? Why can't they understand that what you do is valuable and take better advantage of it? Maybe it's because they don't exactly know what it is that you do.

What do you do?

In a word, lots. But that doesn't define things very finitely for the people with whom you work. Let's circle back to the definition stated in the introduction to this book:

❶ Promoting a healthy body image is among Tri Delta sorority officials' concerns. A strong, sculptural photo delivers the danger of anorexia subtly at first, then strongly as the image becomes more readable with further study.
Art direction/design: Jimmy Ball; photo: Stone

❷ Fire safety is an all-too-familiar topic for collegiate housing specialists, but this dramatic, clutter-free newsletter layout grabs and holds the attention.
Art direction/design: Jimmy Ball; photo: Eyewire

"Being a corporate designer takes up 10 percent of the time. Everything else—managing time, understanding budgets, knowing the product—is the other 90 percent."

Art director of a major California-based internet search engine company

An in-house designer is a professional creative who produces graphic design for, and is an employee of, an organization whose main business is not usually design related.

This definition does not take into account the type of work the designer does, nor does it describe the size or type of organization. Everyone's job is, of course, completely different. It also does not suggest benefit, like this description does:

An in-house designer is a professional creative who enables the organization to communicate with its customers/audience; differentiate, explain, and promote its product or service; and thereby further its means.

In short, the in-house designer is the person who connects the organization to success. Do the people you work with know that? Did you know that?

What do you *not* do?

More specifically, what should you *not* do? Perhaps explaining this to co-workers—and understanding it yourself—will make the definition clearer.

- You are not a service department. It is crucial that you establish yourself within the organization as a design expert, not just a pair of hands waiting to execute other people's bright ideas.

- You are not a miracle worker, nor should you play the hero or martyr. When jobs come in with inadequate resources—information, time, budget, etc.—it's not your responsibility to pull it out of the fire barehanded.

- You should not sit idly by as plum jobs are sent out of house. Again, establishing yourself as the in-house design expert is so important: if work needs to be sent outside, you should be making the decision.

- You should not be an enabler of your employer's bad habits or be a willing victim. If procedure of any kind is making your life or work a misery, it is your responsibility to work to change it.

Again, do your co-workers understand this? How can you explain it? Later chapters of this book will offer concrete methods for preventing all of these situations. For now, we'll speak in broader terms.

1

2

① To avoid yet
another group-shot-with-
oversized-check photo,
designer Jimmy Ball
created a bold, "last-
minute" type treatment,
to stress that fund-
raising was ongoing.
Art direction/design:
Jimmy Ball

② & ③ Jimmy Ball,
graphic designer for the
sorority Delta Delta Delta,
used simple resources to
create this magazine
cover and inside spread
on branding. It's an eye-
catching and easy-to-
understand concept.
Art direction/design/
photography: Jimmy Ball

"A lot of sorority life is fake, I felt.
I'm sure the other girls don't feel like that, but I do.
I felt like I was paying for a brand.
And it is hard for me because I'm not the type to flaunt brands."

The Tri Delta Brand in Action

3

Let's circle back to our definition, taking everything into account:

The in-house designer is the person who connects his or her employer to success by creating original, well-thought-out, informed communications for the organization and who manages time, budget, and other resources in ways that best benefit the organization.

In other words, it's not enough to act as, or be regarded simply as, a creative person. You must also be a very effective manager and leader. Think of it like driving a car: you're bound for trouble if all you do is step on the gas. You absolutely must be able to plan the trip, as well as brake and steer. You have to understand the complete operation of the vehicle.

Case Study **Fossil, Inc.**
Learn Who You Serve

Stephen Zhang is guardian of Fossil's brand identity. As Vice President and Image Director, he is responsible for defining the direction of Fossil's image and for communicating it to anyone who designs and markets the Fossil brand. He manages the Fossil image group, which includes 34 designers.

Since 1984, Fossil has been recognized not only for its exceptional products, but also for the design that supports it. Its graphics and product design are so exceptional that a book was published on them: *Tinspiration*. The graphics team has been recognized by many awards and publication articles over the years.

"When we talk to members of our department about what their role in the company is and to give them perspective, we say this: you have three masters to serve and satisfy at one time:

"1. The brand. We may only be designing a very small tag or adding on to another project, but we are always stacking onto what is already there.

"2. Sales. This requirement must always be fulfilled, or the company ceases to exist.

"3. Design. We have to be able to look at design and see what it can do to improve sales or make the brand clearer. However, the design should never suffer as a result of serving business and brand.

"If we take a single-pronged approach and help sales but do not build the brand, we fail. If we build the brand, but don't help sales, we fail. Design supports both, but in some companies, it is the element that is sacrificed. But if we can serve all three masters, we will build the brand, improve sales, and be creatively satisfied."

1

2

① Spread from Fossil's Brand Book. "It is our tool to communicate our brand essence to all employees and our business contacts. Its format is large so it is effective in presentations at sales conferences," explains Stephen Zhang. *Art director: Stephen Zhang, Evalyn German; designer: Evalyn German; poster graphics designed by Dustin Wallace, Jean Paul Khabbaz, Hyun-Jung Kim, Dru McCabe, Brent Couchman, Rachel Voglewede, Pamela Jackson, Mor Drori*

② The men's leather department at Fossil didn't feel that the tin packaging for its wallets reflected their product's quality. Fossil's design department accepted the challenge: they changed the tins' construction so that they looked cleaner and more sophisticated. Preserving the tin packaging maintains the brand's heritage, explains Stephen Zhang, Vice President and Fossil's Image Director. *Designers: Evalyn German, Jena-Paul Khabbaz; art director: Jon Kirk*

"If we can serve all [our] masters, we will build the brand, improve sales, and be creatively satisfied."

Case Study **Metro**
Leading Change

Michael Lejeune is Creative Director for Metro, the Los Angeles County Metropolitan Transportation Authority, a quasi-governmental agency that provides bus and rail services and plans for future mobility in Southern California. Metro has an annual budget of $3 billion and 9,000 employees.

❶-❹ All Metro advertising is created in-house, which keeps costs down, reports Creative Director Michael Lejeune. Metro employees are used as models, saving even more money. And, by keeping such a fun creative endeavor in-house, the staff continues to enjoy its work.
Photographer: David Zaitz

Lejeune and Lead Designer Neil Sadler lead a remarkable team of eight full-time designers, plus a number of freelancers. The design studio, working alongside Metro's marketing department, has moved from an annual media budget of $300,000 to $3.5 million, due mostly to an in-house "angel" in the form of a Chief Communications Officer who champions their cause. The design studio's work has been featured in *Communication Arts* magazine as well as *Fast Company* magazine. Perhaps even more important, reports Lejeune, design peers outside of the organization have taken notice of their work, and a position in the studio has become a highly sought-after post.

"In 2002, there was a change of guard here. Previously, the organization was commonly known as the MTA—Metropolitan Transportation Authority—which made us sound bureaucratic and not very friendly. The graphics department had fallen under the charge of various areas. At one time, the same people who were in charge of fixing the elevators were also in charge of graphic design.

"There was a bell on the counter where you came into the graphics department. If you needed a brochure, say, you'd come in, ring the bell, hand a designer a disc with text and pictures on it, and tell him that you needed the brochure in two weeks. Then the design person would take the material, put it together, and slap the logo on wherever it seemed to fit—there was little consistency or creative direction. That was it.

"If you don't [have an in-house angel], you have to take the responsibility for finding the change agents, the people who make the decisions that affect what you do."

1

The cure for the common houseguest.

If summer visitors are cramping your style, visit the Trip Planner at metro.net. Then hand 'em a Day Pass and let us drive. They save; you smile. Go Metro.

Ⓜ Metro

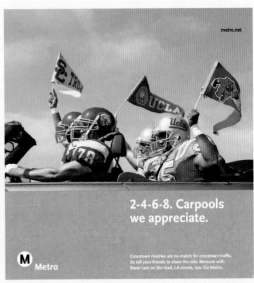

2

2-4-6-8. Carpools we appreciate.

Crosstown rivalries are no match for crosstown traffic. So tell your friends to share the ride. Because with fewer cars on the road, LA scores, too. Go Metro.

Ⓜ Metro

3

Door-to-door service. Well, *almost*.

In the past few years, we've refined routes and added stops to make our bus service more convenient. We can't always promise to drop you at your door, but we're getting closer all the time. Go Metro.

Ⓜ Metro

4

Dash through holiday traffic.

Here's a bright idea for maneuvering a hectic holiday season: Let Metro shuttle out-of-town guests, be your designated driver, or ease your morning commute. For happier holidays, those in the know Go Metro.

Ⓜ Metro

1

2

① A Metro advert in-situ.
Photographer: David Zaitz

② The concept behind this bus tail ad was to present the dangers cyclists face as a series of phobia, presented to help drivers understand the cyclist's point of view as they share the road.

We set up lots of templates for repeating jobs. It took a lot of brainpower in the beginning, but now it is more effortless. We always use the same type and a certain grid system. All of this put the bones in place for our team.

"Now we are doing very high profile work, seen by a large audience. It all adds to our cache as an in-house team, and this helps us to attract a really talented pool of interns and applicants. But it didn't happen all in one day. We do have our in-house champions. But if you don't, you have to take the responsibility for finding the change agents, the people who make the decisions that affect what you do.

"Then you need to lobby for a place at the table, at those meetings where decisions are made. But if you do get that seat, if you finally get into that launch meeting or the new product discussion, or whatever, and can't talk intelligently about the business whose logo is on your paycheck, or tell how your group's skills can benefit the whole organization, you won't be asked back to the table again. You have to immerse yourself in the company's products and business model to be able to generate visual solutions that work.

"When we needed to convince Metro's Board of Directors that it was time for a new logo and new branding, we used visual examples

"Our new CEO brought his marketing chief with him from another large transit company, and things started to change. I was hired as the agency's first Creative Director, and Neil Sadler joined us as Lead Designer. We began to set graphics standards—one typeface, a friendlier tone, logo consistency. At Metro, we're all about safety, reliability, and being on time, so consistency is crucial. The logo has to be in the same place every time. We launched a new advertising campaign and designed new timetables, new tickets, new maps, new bus graphics, everything.

3

4

③ Metro's in-house designers and photographers create covers for the organization's award-winning *Metro Quarterly* news-magazine, which means money isn't being spent on stock photos or custom illustrations. Keeping the work in-house also helps maintain very tight timelines.

④ Metro designers design and place wayfinding signs like this one so that subway passengers can orient themselves the minute they exit a train. By using backlit material like this, the design team can update information at a much lower cost than they can with permanent signs.

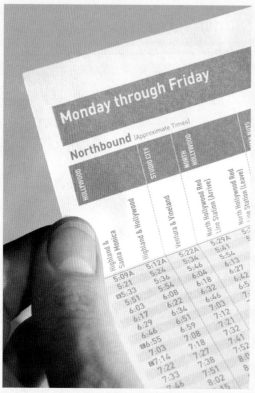

1

2

① Metro designers work with their own print shop, which not only helps them maintain quality, but they can also test ink colors and papers for maximum readability at the lowest cost, as they did with this timetable.

② Creative Director Michael Lejeune says the single most impactful design his team has implemented is the re-imaging of Metro's bus fleet. The formerly white buses blended in with other service vans and trucks on LA's busy streets. Now, bright orange, red, and blue buses catch the eye from blocks away.

of successful competitors to demonstrate why establishing a consistent brand is so important. We showed the Board what Fed Ex has done. For us, Transport for London is another great example: there's a 100-year-old transit system that is still viable and vital.

"If you can show that you understand the business, that you're not some flighty group who doesn't understand the manufacturing process or the sales speech, your ability to garner support greatly increases.

"You have to remember that designers are often viewed with suspicion because people don't understand what we do. We stare at a blank piece of paper, the wheels are turning but are not visible, and then work comes out. On the other hand, everyone likes to 'be creative,' to get involved with what we do. But you often find out that what they really want is control. If you can show people that you are still listening to them and understand what they do, no one gets freaked out.

"It comes down to regarding your organization as a client. This is essential, and our internal system at Metro is set up for that. Our marketing employees function as account executives: they go out and meet with people throughout the company, and then work with us to create the marketing plan or creative brief. That gives us a buffer zone: we don't have people from other departments standing behind our computers asking when that brochure will be done.

"We do have schedules and budgets, and having this formality, where co-workers are clients, creates a more professional exchange when it comes to handling money, timelines, and expectations. Everyone grows to learn that their project can't always be first: they have to get in line. This allows us to handle jobs that take six months and jobs that take 15 minutes and give them all the same amount of respect. Every job, no matter how small, is important to someone at our company.

"Having a collegial but professional way of handling the work promotes order and respect. We are forced to deliver as well: if we don't do what we say, people will mutiny and go outside for their design work. That's not only a loss of resources for the company, it's a loss of control and consistency for the Metro brand."

3

3 Metro designers have the benefit of being able to respond quickly to their customer's reactions. The Metro icon series was originally developed to communicate "no-no" rules to customers. But the icons proved so popular that designers put them on a shirt which is sold through Metro's online store. "Whenever we commission illustration or photography, we work an unlimited-use buyout into the price. Our library of photos and icons can then be used as often as needed, across a variety of formats, without incurring additional costs," explains Michael Lejeune.

4 Each February 14, Metro's design studio crew runs up and down the stairs of the company's headquarters, turning on and off office lights and closing and opening blinds to build this 12-story-high heart as a Valentine's Day present to downtown LA. "It's a no-cost way to send our customers and neighbors some Metro love," says Michael Lejeune.

4

① Metro Lead Designer Neil Sadler put together a comprehensive set of signage guidelines for his organization—an extensive standards manual—that is provided to planners, architects, and builders with whom the organization works. The book protects the brand even when the designers can't be there to defend it.

② A stock photo has cost, but clever and appropriate typography costs nothing.
Art direction/design: Jimmy Ball; photo: Digital Vision

What does your employer do?

Do you really and truly understand the reason your employer exists? Do you know what it actually wants from you? At the most literal level, your employer makes something or performs some sort of service. But if you could speak with the company's founder, you would likely discover that he or she has a larger vision, a big picture for the organization with more noble goals.

At the most basic level, your organization has a model that is mirrored the world round. It has employees, to whom it pays some sort of recompense for their service to the company. So it is somewhat like a machine that must be run in a certain way. There is fuel (wages and shared vision) and there is output (products or service).

The in-house creative person must respect the machinery, no matter how much it drives him or her crazy. Without it, the organization does not function, and the designer (and everyone else) will soon be out of a job. Even the most entrepreneurial company has its cogs that must turn in a certain direction. It's part of the bargain in accepting an in-house position.

So studying the company's design—its structure—is a must. A savvy in-house designer will soon discover who the ultimate decision makers are in the company, and who that person's left- and right-hand people are. Who is (or could be, with encouragement) the champion for design within the organization? Who is the point person?

Once that person or persons has been identified, they are sources from whom to get concrete answers about the brand. Be persistent and ask plenty of questions. Don't make assumptions.

In addition to determining what the organization's long-term, big picture goals and vision are, it's crucial to listen to what the short-term goals and concerns are as well, according to the voices in the trenches. This is where in-house designers can begin to convince the organization that design has real benefit, now and in the future.

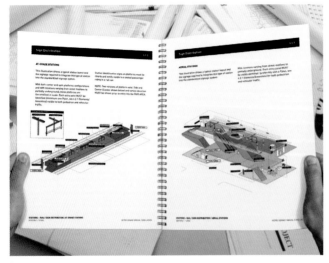

1

Alzheimer's Disease:
A Disconnection

By Jennie Williams Swanson Dincecco, Ed.D.

Case Study **Mutual of Omaha**
It's A Jungle In There

Anne Maguire is the Manager for Graphic Design for Mutual of Omaha, the US insurance company that became known in the 1960s and 70s for the animal and adventure TV show it sponsored, titled *Wild Kingdom*. In fact, most people over age 35 can't even refer to the program so finitely: for them, it's "Mutual of Omaha's *Wild Kingdom*." The show is now back in production under the company's sponsorship. But some employees have trouble disassociating the TV program and the day-to-day realities of business and how design supports sales.

1 This design was created by the in-house team at Mutual of Omaha to advertise a traveling exhibition of historic sports photography that was sponsored by the company. Working closely with the printer and die-maker, the designer was able to showcase the photos which capture the split-second moments that separate the win from the loss. *Designer: Pat Osborne; writer: Mary Maynard*

2 The annual report is always a favorite project for the design team. Each year, the assigned designer travels with the writers and a photographer to locations around the US to meet with the people featured in the report. The week-long odyssey on the corporate jet provides an opportunity for the designer to bring true-to-life stories to the pages of the report. *Designer: Pat Osborne; writers: Sephera Staley, Andy Halperin*

"We are the keepers of the brand. The people who work here are our partners, and Mutual of Omaha is our client. But it wasn't always set up that way.

"Our graphics were a total hodge-podge before. Every division of the company had a different look. When we started our rebranding, we put up all of our brochures and called it the 'Wall of Shame.' We

1

mutual of omaha foundation *impacting lives*

Logan Epp enjoys doing what most kindergartners do – singing songs, giving hugs and playing with his toys. But there's something unique about this happy-go-lucky, energetic 5-year-old.

Watching him walk and talk is like witnessing a miracle.

"He's so full of life for a kid they said would never even get to live," said Logan's mom, Dani Epp. Two weeks after Logan was born, he suffered a seizure and was admitted to Children's Hospital in Omaha, Neb. The doctors diagnosed Logan with Enterovirus Meningitis, an illness that few children Logan's age survive.

Logan spent the next several weeks in the Pediatric Intensive Care Unit on life support. When the doctors were finally able to take an MRI of his brain, the results were devastating.

"The doctors told me that if he did survive, he would probably never breathe on his own, walk, talk or recognize me – and that killed me," Dani said. After much serious thought, Dani and her family made the excruciating decision to take Logan off life support. The hospital staff placed him in her arms and told her that he would likely be gone in a matter of hours.

But Logan refused to give up. Slowly, over the next several weeks, his condition miraculously improved. And, before she knew it, Dani was faced with a new dilemma – she would be taking home a child who would have significant medical needs.

That's when the hospital staff handed Dani a brochure about the Children's Respite Care Center (CRCC) – a nonprofit organization dedicated to providing specialized day services to children with special needs. Supported by the Mutual of Omaha Foundation, CRCC has a staff of dedicated nurses and teachers who are able to provide the kids with medical attention, while also offering multiple services including education, behavior therapy and summer camp.

Thanks to CRCC, Dani was able to keep her job while knowing that Logan was in good hands. Today, Logan attends CRCC in a brand new, state-of-the-art facility that the Mutual of Omaha Foundation helped fund. It's a facility and an organization that Dani credits with Logan's significant growth. "They saved our lives," Dani said.

Helping families like the Epps is the reason the Mutual of Omaha Foundation exists. Through its financial support of nonprofit organizations like CRCC in the Omaha/Council Bluffs metro area, the Foundation is committed to empowering families to overcome obstacles and work toward positive change. Specifically, the Foundation focuses on organizations that directly impact families with the greatest needs in three areas of focus: family health, education and basic human needs.

"What the Mutual of Omaha Foundation does is so necessary," Dani said. "I know firsthand what a difference it makes."

MUTUAL OF OMAHA FOUNDATION'S AREAS OF FOCUS

• Family Health
• Education
• Basic Human Needs

2

① Mutual of Omaha's corporate identity program was designed by award-winning designer Bart Crosby. The company's in-house designers use his guidelines as a framework to manage the brand and create their own award-winning work.
Designer Kerry Stinson; writer Leslie Washburn

"We are the keepers of the brand. The people who work here are our partners."

had meetings with hundreds of people throughout the company to show them the wall and explain why a consistent brand was important. We also wanted to show why having pictures of wild animals on our brochures created a complete disconnect. We needed to show pictures of people on our materials, not a tiger. *Wild Kingdom* is not part of our product promotion.

"Everyone, as they sat in the meetings, was on board with the rebranding. But there were still people in the first year who didn't like the palette we chose or wanted a tiger on their design—but those were the people who were used to treating our department as order takers. We had to keep showing

them the *business* reason behind why a photo or color wouldn't work, and we showed them how every time they came in to make changes or suggestions, they were increasing cost and work for the company.

"But it's not just one-sided. The first Friday of every month, we invite people from different parts of the company to come speak to us about what they do and what their goals are. That's how we get educated. We also put our designers through a course on presentation, so the person who creates the work also presents the work. The account executives aren't the only ones who have contact with the larger company."

1

What does your employer want *you* to do?

Too many companies treat their design departments like production houses: all hands, no brains. In these organizations, people want to enter the department, place their order, and want the designer to plop the order on the tray. It's a bit like McDonald's. One doesn't want to engage the kid behind the counter in a discussion about the preparation of the fries. We just want them and we want them fast.

Of course, this creates a pretty joyless existence for the designer. At some point, the order-after-order mentality has to be changed. Co-workers have to be shown, through the designer's actions, that a much better product—and sometimes, better price and schedule—can be delivered.

Employer or client?

For the in-house designer, it's an ongoing conundrum. Some prefer to regard their employer as just that—an employer. But for others, it helps to maintain more of an outside perspective. In later chapters, we'll share techniques for managing budgets, time accounting systems, and other structures that can help you quantify and keep track of resources.

But for now, consider another position: it is possible to regard yourself as a diagnostician. That is, you help your employer/client define particular problems or needs and then help it find the best solution.

Be an advocate for design: it's a simple statement, but as you know, it's also a full-time job. It's a job that will be much easier if you can, through your work as a diagnostician, position yourself as the design and creative expert within your organization.

2

2 Frequency North is an aggressively eclectic visiting writer's reading series at The College of Saint Rose. The College's designers created this compelling poster that reflects the nature of the events.
Art director/designer: Mark Hamilton; writer/project manager: Daniel Nester

1

1 Transit ads reach young, potential college students where they live: out and about, on the town. These bus banners, for The College of Saint Rose, take advantage of the high penetration of outdoor advertising in the Albany area.
Mark Hamilton; designer/ photographer: Chris Parody; writer: Lisa Haley Thomson, John Backman; project manager: Lisa Haley Thomson

2 Designer Jimmy Ball snipped the cookie cutter and shot the photo for this magazine contents page, an extremely low-cost way to visually make a point.
Art direction/design/ photography: Jimmy Ball

Becoming known as the "authority" is accomplished through building trust relationships with people. That's one of the enormous benefits of working in in-house design—the opportunity to develop long-term relationships. But simply being friendly is not enough. You must show that your contribution to the larger organization is not only important, but crucial to everyone's success.

For instance, it is not enough to simply tell someone that a certain color or typeface "won't work." You must, instead, tell them why—and sometimes you will end up explaining this again and again.

Even beyond the reason why, you must explain the benefit of that decision. "That face won't work in that size as it will be too small to read on the website, and if people can't read the type, they won't know how to proceed to ordering," might be a fully played out version of one instance. If this does not convince a co-worker, you may have to present more options and examples.

The key is to show that you have the other person's best interests at heart, as well as those of the company. You are a partner not only to those around you, but to the company as well.

The Recruitment Issue

Case Study Fossil, Inc.
At The Heart Of Business

More from Fossil's Stephen Zhang, this time on discovering the vision that lies at the heart of any company.

"In the past few years, we have worked on the company's vision and values. At one point, there was an active discussion of what Fossil is all about. When they were asked what the company's mission statement was, one group from sales stated it in terms of its department goals: to become a $2 billion company. But the CEO reminded us of why the company was started in the first place: a group of interesting people got together to put forth their point of view through design. We want to enjoy what we do—design vintage, surprising, and artistic goods, and if we get to $2 billion in the meantime, fine. If not, we had fun. For me, that really put into perspective what we do."

❶ Always vintage-inspired, the in-house Fossil team looks for ways to redefine the brand in more culturally and design-relevant terms. In this case, the designer/illustrator, Ellen Tanner, took vintage clippings from old magazines and illustrated on and around them to create a completely new context. This technique was subsequently utilized across a number of projects, including a very successful annual report design.

1

Case Study **Nickelodeon**
Expert Care

Rohat Cellali-Sik is off-air graphic designer for Nickelodeon in the UK: in fact, he is the only print designer in the building. His company is a tempting target for outside design and ad agencies: who wouldn't want Nickelodeon on their CV? Outside account executives are constantly wooing decision-makers there. But Cellali-Sik works steadily to demonstrate that in-house is the best choice for his company.

"Agencies might have a glitzy front door and a receptionist, and they might take you out to lunch or make impressive presentations. But they charge lots to do what I do for a fraction of the cost. And sometimes they return with work that is appalling or which breaks our style guides. We end up patching things up in-house.

"We work here full-time and know the brand and how it works. Agencies have so many clients: we only have one—our company. We created the brand—every squiggle of it. How could an agency know the brand as well as we do?

"So we need for people to feel confident coming to us. It should be like coming in to get fitted for a tailor-made suit. There is no clock running when they sit down with me. We ask what they need. We show them things we have done before, or maybe we look at other designers' work to help discussions. I talk to them about actual costs, how if they go outside, the agencies mark up the work. The agencies might pull the wool over my co-workers' eyes, but we know the game. We have to tell them what the real cost is. When you show that you can be smart with ideas and with their purse, then they trust you."

"When you show that you can be smart with ideas and with their purse, then they trust you."

Case Study Whirlpool, Inc.
A Meaningful Role

Brian Edlefson is Art Director for Whirlpool, Inc. He has a great deal of experience as an in-house designer, having worked at Target, Herman Miller, and the Museum of Modern Art in New York City prior to accepting his current position. His success has come from a realistic but practical big-picture view of himself as a design diagnostician.

1 The original Kitchen Aid iconography was compiled piecemeal over time; little consideration was given to the set as a whole. Whirlpool's in-house designers developed an updated visual language that more clearly resonated with the brand. "The in-house design department was in a unique position to identify the problem, complete a visual audit, and create a holistic solution that was appropriate to the brand," explains Lead Graphic Designer Mark Cook.
GCD staff of Whirlpool Corporation

"Mine is a territorial role. When you work for a large company, you can't touch everything that the company does, but I do feel I am responsible for a cohesive thread. I can see what builds a cohesive brand or story for the company.

"Another important thing I do is to help define the process of design. How can design contribute here? How can talents be used, and how can teams be organized? A lot of what I do now is posing options for the company and putting hypotheses out there. I consider how design decisions can impact the face of the organization to the public, and how we can better work together with our business partners.

"It comes down to advocating design every day."

"You can't touch everything that the company does, but I do feel I am responsible for a cohesive thread."

1 & **2** While most college publications are brochures, the design team at The College of Saint Rose created a remarkable case-bound book with matte black foil stamping on raw board for a cover. Red kivar tape is used on the spine. This, combined with the beautifully designed, 100-page interior, depicts the college as distinctive and extraordinary. "The book is designed so as to make the reader pause and to reflect the desire to be more than they are today," explains Art Director and designer Mark Hamilton.

Designer/photo illustrator: Chris Parody; writers: Lisa Haley Thomson, Mary Grondahl; photography: Greg Cherin Photography, Gary Gold Photography, Chris Parody, Mark Hamilton

1

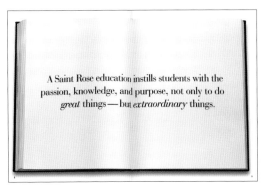

A Saint Rose education instills students with the passion, knowledge, and purpose, not only to do *great* things — but *extraordinary* things.

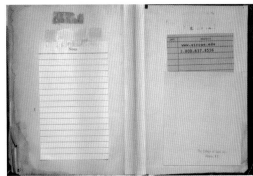

PAINTS WORD PICTURES.

SAINT ROSE GIVES TOAN TRAN THE FREEDOM TO EXPLORE THE *LOOK* OF LANGUAGE.

PASSION. KNOWLEDGE. PURPOSE.

WRITES POETRY ABOUT A BAND.

PROFESSOR DANIEL NESTER WRITES ABOUT "QUEEN." IN HIS CLASSROOM, YOU WRITE ABOUT YOU.

PASSION. KNOWLEDGE. PURPOSE.

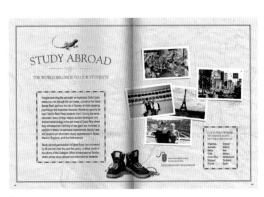

STUDY ABROAD

THE WORLD BELONGS TO OUR STUDENTS

Case Study Lomographic Society International
A Powerful Partner

Sally Bibawy is architect and director of international brand and product development for Lomographic Society International, a company dedicated to the continued study and use of analog photography. She works in Vienna, Austria.

1 The Lomographic Society decided to build its own in-house design department a few years ago for a couple of reasons. First, everyone on the team is a dedicated Lomographer, so they are able to create designs and influence product development in ways that best suit this unique form of analog photography. Second, their appreciation of the photography is clearly communicated in the joy and personality of the company's designs.
Lomographic Society International

"First of all, and most importantly to creative people, is to understand a big organization as a partner. Creative thinking does not mean that you have to fight against a large economic organization, but to understand it as a possible partner in realizing your creative ideas. Therefore, you need to accept your responsibilities.

"Gaining respect in this game means being happy to take responsibility, to constantly update yourself about production and logistical processes, about needs and specialties of different markets, and most important, to be open to limitations without losing the initial creative idea.

"It also means [being willing] to accept communication rules. Without these, the organization would not be able to exist.

"In our company's strategy, the most important role of all people involved in the creative process is to ensure that concept and design always play a major role in the overall structure. The biggest challenge of being an in-house designer is to keep the balance between creative ideas and economic needs. The Lomographic Society, as a company, encourages its designers to always question and control the realization process, especially when it comes to production.

"It is the creative team's role to ensure the best realization. Everybody has his own responsibility in the overall project. Everybody is an important part of the structure, even if he only plays a tiny role in it."

1

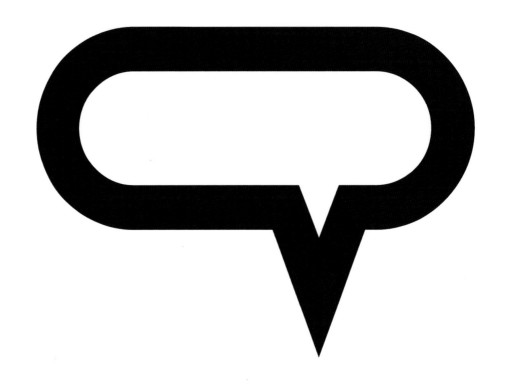

2

In-House Design in Practice

Selling Your Services

Elsa and Rob had been listening to the head of product development for nearly an hour. With the new product launch looming, he had come equipped with a lengthy PowerPoint, a flipchart, and plenty of ideas for the new brochure he wanted.

"If we make it slightly oversized, it will stick up a bit in lit racks. Is it possible to get the logo die-cut into the cover?" he asked enthusiastically. Clearly, he had been thinking about the brochure for a long time. The two designers had taken page after page of notes. "Yes," said Elsa, "but..."

"But what?" The manager stopped in mid-chart flip.

"I think you would get a better return by spending your budget on a website," Elsa replied. Rob nodded. "A website?" the manager asked, looking doubtful. "In fact, for the same money, we can get you a website with a downloadable brochure. It won't be die-cut, but the customer will be able to place their order on the spot," Rob smiled.

"Keep talking," said the manager.

How do you explain what you do?

"Design is a profession based on conception: on helping to define an opportunity, then developing a solution that will fulfill it." (What Every Business Needs, AIGA)

Trying to describe what a designer does—how the creative process works—to a left-brained person is like trying to capture water in your hands: it slips away faster than it can be studied. A cup is much more practical. Similarly, when talking about design with non-creative types, focusing on practical, non-artistic issues also works better. In this way, the actual, swirly nuances of creativity (that with which only the designer is interested) are kept out of the conversation, and focus is placed on the end goal (which everyone is interested in).

General Project Process

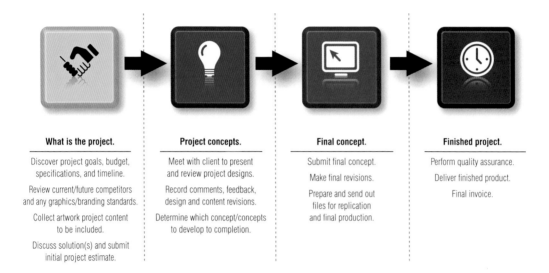

What is the project.	Project concepts.	Final concept.	Finished project.
Discover project goals, budget, specifications, and timeline.	Meet with client to present and review project designs.	Submit final concept.	Perform quality assurance.
Review current/future competitors and any graphics/branding standards.	Record comments, feedback, design and content revisions.	Make final revisions.	Deliver finished product.
Collect artwork project content to be included.	Determine which concept/concepts to develop to completion.	Prepare and send out files for replication and final production.	Final invoice.
Discuss solution(s) and submit initial project estimate.			

1

For example, instead of describing a typeface as more elegant or exciting, the end result is underlined by deeming it more readable or attention-grabbing. A color isn't selected because someone likes it. Instead, it is chosen because it supports the brand. Aesthetics, no. Results, yes.

"The fluid nature of the creative process is hard for a person who uses rules and strict guidelines to direct his daily work activity to understand," explains Mike Soward, an in-house designer with Accretia, a stone and tile flooring company.

But the individual steps of the creative process are important, too: they are how the designer reaches the apex of what is possible. And non-creative people just don't know what's possible. They can't comprehend how the designer's brain works; they don't know what the options are; and they don't understand how the technology the designer uses works.

This does not mean that it is impossible to put onto paper or screen a diagram that explains—in very basic terms—the actual steps a project goes through once it enters the design department. But this

❶ Ken Bullock, Senior Web/Multimedia Designer with KBR Energy and Chemicals, a division of Halleburton, has, over the course of his career as an in-house designer and consultant, developed this simple flow chart to explain what happens to projects once they enter his area. He calls it "The Four D's of Design."

A. Deciding on Colors

Most of the time we are not sure what are the right colors for a logo, brochure or a newsletter. We are unaware of color sensitivity to certain cultures and how color affects our message. This technique will show you how to make use of your photos to determine these colors.

Technique: Pixelate or Mosaic a photo or a set photos in Adobe Photoshop* to 30 square, cell size. The result will be color swatches from your images.

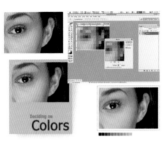

*If you don't have a copy of Adobe Photoshop. Open source software called The Gimp has similar Photoshop effects. You can get a copy at www.gimp.org

B. Guardian of the Grid

All designers and printers rely measuring systems to plan layouts for print. Preparing a document for desktop publishing or offset printing needs the same sort system or discipline.

Technique: Use reference points for text and image placements on layouts. Doing so creates an invisible grid that shows balance and harmony on your layouts.

Practice makes perfect: Try turning on the grid when using your desktop publishing software. Turn on "Snap to Grid" and always use "Guidelines".

C. Text Smart

Type is important because it's an unconscious persuader. It attracts attention, sets the style and tone of a document, and defines the feeling of the page—usually without the reader recognizing a particular typeface.

Technique: Use **Sans Serif for Headlines and Titles**. They usually Bold and Heavy and attract attention. **Use Serif Fonts or typefaces with tails on heavy and lengthy texts.** The conventional wisdom is that serifs help guide the eye along the lines.

Changing Standards: Currently there are no norms in using fonts esp. in electronic media or sometimes even in print.

Research/Google it!: Get to know the fonts you use. Font creators make them for specific purposes. Some fonts are for Newspaper and some are for Magazines. Visit www.fontbureau.com

D. Space not waste

White space should not be considered merely as 'blank' space - it is an important element of design which enables the objects in it to exist at all, the balance between positive (or none-white) and the use of negative spaces is key to aesthetic composition.

Technique: Use photos that have a lot of empty blank spaces. Layout your page with all elements in the center leaving spaces on both sides (see image).

Try it for yourself: Take a sheet of plain paper, and write several lines of text from one edge of the page to the other, without leaving any space at the top or the left and right margin. Now take another sheet of paper and right in the middle, write a few lines of text right in the middle, leaving a generous amount of white space on all sides. Now compare the two pages. Which one is easier to read?

F. Tell a Story

The key is making sure that your photograph tells the story that you have in mind. Of course this can be pretty subjective too because an identical image can mean different things to different people but at the least IT TELLS A STORY.

Telling a story through a detail photo...

Create curiosity!

Black / white always work!

Technique: Avoid taking photos that is conventional and straightforward. Make room for intrigue and curiosity. Photo interpretation is subjective after all captions; headlines and articles always explain the photo.

Technique: Experiment on taking photos with perspectives and angels. Use the MACRO feature of your camera to focus on detail.

"A picture paints a thousand words"

❶ & ❷ Oliver Kuy, an in-house designer for four different companies in the Philippines—he reports to each one separately for one day per week—created a presentation that outlined basic design principles such as use of color, text, space, and grids, for his colleagues. Samples of this are shown here. It was received so well that it is now used by one company, Getz Pharma, for decision-making on design issues.

guide to working with creative team

don't argue with creative team about fonts, colors and other design decisions

do drive your creative team; push us to be more creative, not less.

don't bypass your coordinator

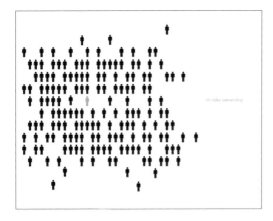

do take ownership

do work hard to understand what creative people are proposing

don't give comments just to give comments

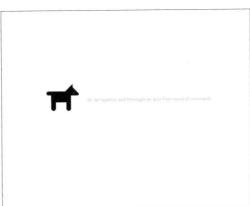

do be rigorous and thorough on your first round of comments

do know what you are aiming for

don't invoke internal politics for reason of doing/not doing something

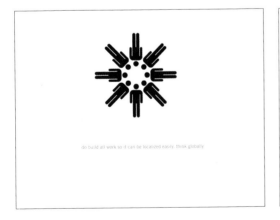

do build all work so it can be localized easily. think globally

be willing to take a chance. be open to unexpected. joke...

"Co-workers often want to include too much information or try to eliminate white space. I ask them what they look at first when they read the Sunday comics. Almost all will respond that they first look at the ones that contain interesting pictures and little text. I tell them to approach their own projects the same way."

Erik Borreson, Senior Graphic Design Specialist at Marshfield Clinics, with 40 locations and 7,000 employees in Wisconsin

must be boiled down to its essence: Its only job is to describe the very rudimentary structure of what is to most an invisible and mysterious process toward a satisfactory end.

Everyone's a designer

As nebulous as the process is to most people, paradoxically, almost everyone fancies him- or herself to be a designer. It's a job that looks fun, so really, how hard could it be? "Let's make the logo lots bigger— in orange!" an assistant from accounting might suggest. You cringe. But whether you agree or not, it is still important to listen to these opinions.

"I might explain that if I make the logo bigger, it will compete with the headline, which is the thing we want the customer to see first," says Irina Blok, who has served as a designer for Yahoo!, LVMH, and several other large media companies. An answer phrased like this addresses the practical nature of the request: it explains how the change would adversely affect the desired end result. But Blok says there is more to consider. "We have

to understand why they are making the request. What do they really want? We have to make choices that everyone is comfortable with."

Pamela Fogg, Art Director for Middlebury College agrees. "We can't have everyone in the admissions office helping us, or the project will turn into a great big camel. But if we do not respect their opinions, we will be off-target and they will not respect our work. You have to show yourself to be a partner," she says.

But you're the expert

You also have to show yourself to be the expert: others may have opinions, but you have the actual working knowledge to get things done correctly. Back up your expertise with the information that only you have access to, such as your past training, color forecasts, design books and magazine articles, design seminar notes, design blogs and sites, and trend surveys. Such sources remove personal biases, and they introduce an outside "expert" to the conversation, in the event you aren't being regarded as such.

The right software is another element that sets designers apart. While most businesspeople today understand and use the Microsoft Suite of products, they do not have the Adobe Suite. They may be good with PowerPoint, but a designer can create a much smoother and agreeable presentation in InDesign. Industry offset printers simply don't support files produced in Word. Like the carpenter, the designer is distinguished as an expert by his tools.

Another way to help others understand what you do and gain their respect as the expert is by simply taking away the headaches. For example, most laypeople have no idea of how printing processes work, but they know a bad job when they see it—and likely have been at the receiving end of one. If the in-house designer can step in and just "handle it," most are more than willing to let him have at it.

What is your mission?

It's tough to explain what you do to others if you're not quite sure yourself. Take the time to develop a department "mission statement" that aligns with the company's mission statement. Clearly define why you are there to yourself. This might be just a sentence or two that simply helps you maintain focus, but it's also something that can be shared with others.

Keep your mission statement simple and positive. "Our department is the guardian and gardener for the brand," is a rather poetic instance. But if such creative-speak is likely to throw colleagues into a left-brained tizz, be more pragmatic:

❶ & ❷ (previous pages) "I have a fun guide to working with creative people," says designer and art director Irina Blok. "People respond to rules, and these rules reveal the process and how to get the best success from design. All of them are written in the client's language, not designer language." Blok's collection of Do's and Don'ts includes advice such as "Don't argue with the creative team about fonts, colors, and other design decisions" and "Do know what you are aiming for."

❶ (this page) Nina Kulhawy, Senior Designer with the Provost Communications Group at Arizona State University, developed this presentation for co-workers not only to explain the value of design, but also to help others understand how they can get the best results while working with a designer.

Color is relative

Color is cultural

Color is emotional

If you were a typeface,
what would you be?

I've got a feeling we're
not in 1994 anymore.

Mi hex code es su hex code.

You had me at Perpetua.

Love is blind.
Our audience isn't.

Love means never
having to redesign.

DPI, PPI, CMYK, RGB, PMS, EPS,
CSS, HTML, WYSIWYG, FTP, GIF,
TIF, PDF, PNG, PHP, URL.

ASU

Carpe Sparkem.

I feel the need,
the need for *Frutiger.*

*"Nobody puts
Sparky
in the corner!"*
–Johnny

Unless it looks good.

Completely FAT FREE.

*Dear Sparky,
Do you like me?*
YES   NO

circle one
NO MAYBES!!!

But it's a dry maroon.

Be part of the
Law and Order:
Special Visual Unit.

I dream in maroon and gold.

My midnight oil is
Pantone 123.

That's hot.

Now with added
SPARKOSITY!

Logo-licious.

These colors won't even melt in
your hands.

Sunshine
365 days a year.

"We maintain and develop the brand according to the company's changing needs." Whatever you come up with, be sure to get buy-in from higher-ups to be certain that your vision and theirs mesh.

But don't limit your statement just to design issues. The in-house designer must also consider his other crucial role—that of the comrade-in-arms who can actively participate in organizational discussions that may not relate directly to design. In order to be perceived as an equal partner, sitting on one's hand during a meeting won't work.

Show *and* tell

However you explain what you do, remember that most people are not as visual as you are. Verbally describing your vision of a website may work when you are speaking to another designer. But even if a non-designer is nodding enthusiastically, he likely is not getting an accurate picture. Always provide images, even if they are only basic sketches, in color, if possible. It may slow down your process terribly to produce a tight comp, but in the end, it may be worth it to get an accurate reaction from the client.

"I always show people what I do rather than try to explain it," says designer Guy Kelly of F+W Publications. "I get involved in early proposals of books, set up mid-point meetings with the editorial

department, and offer direction wherever I can. Through this process, I show what the designer's role is, and it's not just arranging art in a pretty way."

It also makes a lot of sense to bring in work that other designers, outside of your organization, have done. Spread plenty of exemplary design samples out on the table and ask the client what he or she likes or doesn't like. Ask why or why not. Ask them to bring in work that they like as well. Point out those companies which maintain brand standards well—Apple, for instance—and explain how they do it. Most people can appreciate good design once it's laid squarely in front of them.

① & **②** Nina Kulhawy of Arizona State University produced a series of somewhat irreverent cards which she and others in her office can give to colleagues to promote the university's online communications guide, which helped to keep everyone on the same page brand-wise. The emphasis was on team-building, not rule-giving.

"You can love your job, but it will never love you back."
Mary Ridgway, Art Director for University Relations, Fort Hays State University

2

Case Study **Virgin Atlantic**
Innovation, Innovation, Innovation

Joe Ferry is in the enviable position of heading up the design department at Virgin Atlantic, an innovative London-based airline well-known for its attention to detail and to its customers. His philosophy is that through constant product, service, and graphic design innovation, the future of the company is ensured.

"Everyone in the organization is my customer, and we are here to provide customer service."

1

"A key thing that we avoid is talking about aesthetics to people not immediately associated with design. They may already think of us as stylists or as superficial. Instead, we talk about the commercial side of things. If we do graphics for a clubhouse, we don't say, 'Doesn't it look great?' We explain how we have expanded the capacity of the space on a reduced budget.

"Always come at it from the viewpoint of the benefits that you can bring to the commercial side of the company. What sorts of buzzwords can you use to generate interest with the particular person you are addressing? With accounting people, talk about budget efficiencies, for example.

"You really have to be quite sympathetic to all of the needs of the company but still push for innovation. We have to collaborate with the people who implement our designs as well as the people who live with them day in and day out. You end up being everyone's best friend—although right before something is launched, my name is usually mud. Everyone in the organization is my customer, and we are here to provide customer service.

"I could say, 'Wouldn't it be wonderful to put a four-poster bed on board for every passenger?' and it would be, but that doesn't serve the company well. We would lose too many seats. But maybe we as designers can think of another innovation—create the kind of bed that does work. We are still giving excellent customer service, but are pushing the boundaries of design.

"What keeps us excited is knowing that what we are working on really will go live eventually. With an outside design firm, the client always has control. Here, we have far more control of getting product to market."

❶–❸ Virgin Atlantic is credited with inventing the truly accommodating business lounge. Not only are amenities considerate and well-thought-out, the lounges are also just plain beautiful, thanks to the company's design teams. "In our 12 to 13 years of existence, we have managed to explain the importance of design in business innovation," says Joe Ferry. Shown here is London's Heathrow clubhouse.

2

3

○ ○ ○   MNI – What Is MNI? – Direct response PostIt Notes

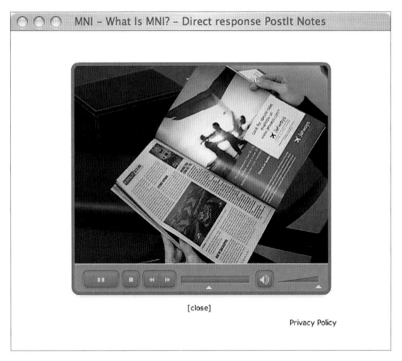

[close]

Privacy Policy

1 To promote Media Network's direct response products on the company's website, MNI's creative staff wrote the copy, designed the set, created the storyboards, and filmed and designed the interface for an online Flash movie. It saved the company money and helped expand the creative team's skill set.
Creative team: Rachel Rowan, Aesha Sharrieff, Mindi Lund, Keri Thomas, Courtney French

○ ○ ○   MNI – What Is MNI? – Direct response PostIt Notes

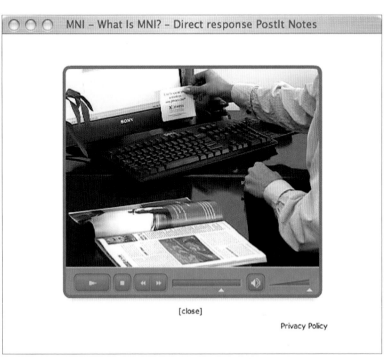

[close]

Privacy Policy

How do you explain your tools?

Some in-house designers find it helpful to explain their tools—software, mood boards, type, etc.—to co-workers, while others believe it unnecessarily muddies the waters, taking the focus off of the ultimate goal: a successful design. A common ground, it seems, is a brand standards manual. However modest, this should lay out preapproved parameters—color, typestyle, grid, and more—in a bible-like form against which most people won't argue.

"We have an established brand standards guide that we refer to whenever questions arise. We have specific fonts that we don't stray from, and that helps our brand maintain consistency in the marketplace. With new retail competition appearing, it's more important than ever to have a recognizable brand look and feel," explains Erin Smithmier, a designer with Helzberg Diamonds. "It's impossible to have in-house and external designers all working on projects using their own fonts, colors, and so on. The guide acts as a traveling enforcer of the work we've put into making our brand consistent."

But those outside of the department must be aware that the standards manual exists. The designer may need to conduct training meetings with managers, provide copies for

"Sometimes when I really get ticked off at my boss, I email him a message in all uppercase script font just to prove a point."

In-house designer with a large, multi-city architectural firm

easy reference, create an online version for even quicker reference, be responsible for updating and evolving the guide, and provide examples of designs that have been created using the standards.

Of course, standards manuals don't create themselves: it all points toward more work for the already harried in-house designer. But the upfront legwork will prevent hours and hours of aggravation later.

Jargon

You may not think your tools are all that confusing, but to the layperson, talking about "figure-ground reversal" is jargonism and exclusionary. "White space" is much more inclusive. Whenever possible, use clear language—"header font" as opposed to "sans serif copy," or "color matching inks" rather than "PMS." In other words, speak their language whenever possible.

Explain your work's value

Sometimes proving value in your work is a matter of gaining respect among peers or satisfying internal ROI requests; sometimes, though, it can protect you against downsizing. Seeing actual value is also important to you, too, as an individual, to prevent burn-out and discouragement.

"When things in Silicon Valley were first beginning to explode, a manager I was working with realized that the blood, sweat, and tears of his software engineers would mean nothing if what they were producing was not presented in an engaging way through design. They realized that sex sells; technology does not. Designers have the ability to think in the abstract, so our process is actually very harmonious to the engineering process. There is a huge value in that."

Michele Floriani, Director of Branding, BMC Software

But how to measure value? Design is not something you can count. There are common sense methods that are convincing, however.

- Just plain save them money. While Art Director at Yahoo!, Irina Blok was asked by the human resources department to create a new folder in which to send documents. Instead of just blindly giving the client what he wanted, Blok considered what the customer's experience would be with the folder. "I found out they were sending out six different packages already, and a seventh would not be a good idea," she says. Her idea was to combine all of the mailers into one and make it very special. "We created a purple self-mailer box—that's the corporate color—that yodels. It had all of the fun of the company, was a huge hit, gave us a huge cost savings, and upped response by 20 percent. Creative people have the power to apply special thinking to business problems. We're not just order takers."

- When you save the client money, let everyone know through a company newsletter or a quick emailed note. But give credit to every department and individual who was involved, inside and outside of the design department. Likely you can't take the sole credit.

- Add up what the cost would have been for specific assignments if they had been sent to an outside agency. Compare those numbers to your budget. The cost-savings (and likely, time-savings, too) will be immediately evident.

- Track projects. Growth in numbers and of complexity of projects are signs that the overall organization is being well served by your design. Share those numbers with your managers so that they have the information they need to secure additional resources for your group. Look for other ways to measure your design's influence. The effect of a PR program, for instance, might be difficult but not impossible to gauge. Has attendance at company-sponsored events increased? Do the number of calls coming in spike during the weeks following a program's release? Measurements may not be scientific, but they will show results. Most organizations have in-house accounting departments: ask someone within that group to help you interpret

1

or present numbers in a way that other number-crunchers in the company will best understand.

- Enter design competitions. Outside recognition can carry a lot of weight with administrators who aren't able to gauge the merit of design. It shows that others believe you are doing a good job.

- Save thank-you notes or other correspondence that praises your work. Have such documentation at the ready at annual review or budget time.

- Host your own show. "Our team advertises our services to the rest of the company," says John Jones, a graphic design specialist with Southwest Airlines. "We recently held a design show in one of the training rooms here at headquarters. We invited all of our current clients and sent invitations—by email, to keep

❶ The "Advance Way Brand Book" was produced entirely in-house by Advance Auto designers Ann Clayton and Marcie Phoebus. Distributed at a leadership development conference for managers, it highlights each team member's role in the proper use and care of the company's brand.

1 The iSite Employee Resource CD was developed by Deloitte & Touche's (now just Deloitte) in-house design department. The Lead Designer, Ken Bullock, designed the project to replace the existing orientation pack for new employees, which was a four inch (10cm) thick binder with hundreds of sheets of paper. The CD is easily updated, actively linked to the company intranet for the latest content, delivers significant cost-savings, is more convenient to carry, and is far more user-friendly.
Designer/art director: Ken Bullock; human resources manager: Cindy Creeden; designers: Denise Whitton, Doug Allen

costs down—to all executive assistants. At the show, all work was mounted on black board. By taking this extra step, we look more professional and it helps us to be seen as designers, rather than the Kinko's production team." Jones' group also ran a projected presentation with more examples of their work together with quotes from satisfied customers. Simple refreshments were served and hip, loungy music played in the background. The event was well attended and the feedback great. "We got lots of comments like, 'I didn't know you guys did that project,' and 'You guys can do that?'" he says.

■ Not every company can be the market leader. If you're employed by an organization that is currently or constantly outpaced by competitors, you've actually been presented with an excellent opportunity to prove your work's value. Point out new directions where the organization might change. Focus on market/product innovation and differentiation. It's the design team's role to show how much commercial benefit can be made through design.

How the client obtains value

Consider the following list. If an in-house designer is not receiving any one of these items from the larger organization, his or her work will suffer. Take immediate measures to secure the missing element.

■ Trust: you need to have the authoritative trust of not just the managers, but of everyone else in the company as well. Fortunately for the designer, branding is now the higher calling in the corporate world, and the in-house designer is the brand's single greatest advocate. The company must respect that—and you. Nevertheless, respect is something you have to earn over time—sometimes over lots of time.

■ Time: it's very rare that the in-house designer has the luxury of being able to focus on just one project at a time. And it's a difficult conversation when one must tell a colleague that there simply was not enough time to complete a particular project: he blames you for that problem, not the company. In truth, it may not be the designer's fault, but it is his problem to solve. So how do you eke out more time? Getting more time takes time: provide effective design. Earn more respect. Get longer timelines.

"When I was hired for my first job, my employer wasn't interested in my background or education, only what software I knew how to use. That should have been a warning sign to me. All I could do was the best work I could. Turnaround was very fast—they weren't interested in design concepts, just in cranking it out. But whenever I could, I did my best, and over time, that impressed them. It earned me respect, brought in new revenue for the company, and opened up more opportunities for design."

Guy Kelly, Designer, now at F+W Publications

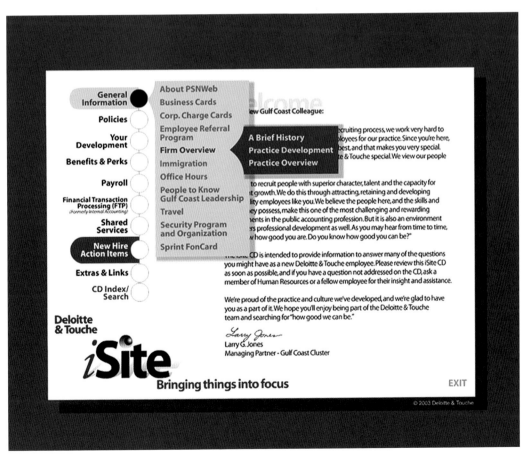

① How could Yahoo! bring the internet to people attending the Olympics? Irina Blok developed a hot dog cart-like contraption that did just that, pulling together resources with which she had never before worked. "Designers can block themselves—they feel they never get any fun projects. That's self-destructive. Propose something fun yourself," she says.

Art director: Irina Blok; design manager: Glenn Tokunaga; marketing manager: Sean Florio, Yahoo!; marketing director: Luanne Calvert, Yahoo!

1

"I struggled with being reactive in my first months. The company had never had a designer before, and they thought I could spit out projects in a matter of hours. Getting a project request form in place solved part of that, and I also had the opportunity to speak at a monthly department head meeting so I could explain how long certain projects take. But a few rebellious people found out the hard way that I wouldn't drop everything to handle their project. One project came in that had to be turned around in less than a week. I simply told them no. I told them I'd be happy to do it when my schedule freed up and I gave them the names of local design firms who might help. They learned and didn't do it again."

Designer for a large restaurant chain

Repeat. It all takes patience—and toughness. Uninterrupted time is also always in notoriously short supply. Designers find it by working evenings or weekends—not problematic perhaps in the short-term, but highly erosive over long stretches of time. The gift of flexible hours and/or being able to work at home is another time-based perk that the organization can offer.

- Direct communication: this means that the in-house designer must be welcome at the conference table. It also means that outside colleagues must honor the forms and requests for information that the design department issues.

- Space: designers need more specialized space for their work, where mock-ups, mood boards, idea boards, and more can be

2 To promote Yahoo!
Shopping, Irina Blok
created the world's
biggest snow globe,
complete with Christmas
scene and Santa. But she
didn't stop her efforts
there: She also worked
closely with a local PR
firm to get the most bang
and coverage for the
company's buck.
Art director: Irina Blok;
copywriter: Vanessa Bauch;
creative manager: Lee
Solon; creative director:
Luanne Calvert

2

Loving Kansas City
for more than 90 years.

Helzberg Diamonds was founded in Kansas City in 1915, and since then we've been a cornerstone of the community. Like Starlight Theatre, we've brought beauty, laughter and sparkle to the people of Kansas City for many generations ... and we look forward to doing so for many years to come.

HELZBERG DIAMONDS
moments that sparkle®

helzberg.com | 800-HELZBERG | 800-435-9237

COUNTRY CLUB PLAZA • INDEPENDENCE CENTER • LEGENDS AT VILLAGE
WEST • METRO NORTH MALL • NORTH KANSAS CITY • OAK PARK MALL
SUMMIT WOODS CROSSING • TOWN CENTER PLAZA • ZONA ROSA

2

❶ Working with a minimal budget, the in-house design group at Helzberg Diamonds produced six different Mother's Day cards and envelopes that would be given to anyone making a purchase during the company's Mother's Day campaign. The project was completed within budget, provided customers with a purchasing incentive, and added value to the company's product.
Designer: Erin Smithmier; CD: Tracie Carvat; copywriter: Sonya Terjanian

❷ Cheap, fast, or good? With in-house design, it's possible to get all three sometimes. Erin Smithmier of Helzberg Diamonds says that this countersign was ordered the same day it was needed. The deadline was met because the design team had immediate access to a well-organized brand library.
Designer: Erin Smithmier; CD: Tracie Carvat; copywriter: Sonya Terjanian

"At one place I worked, it was horrible: I was interrupted all of the time. I was always losing my train of thought. The brand manager and the creative director became my bodyguards. People actually weren't allowed to talk to me for a while. It was just a matter of retraining people."
Cora Lanier, Senior Graphic Designer, Shamir Insight

strokes
of genius
the best of drawing

Edited by Rachel Rubin Wolf

posted. Usually, such "decoration" is in direct violation with company policies on keeping a tidy workspace, but the space is important, nevertheless. A library area with a table is also very helpful for storing the magazines and books that help keep designers informed and competitive. Ideally, the design department and its library will be centrally located within the organization's building: in this way, design remains physically visible all of the time. "Space" can also be defined more broadly. The organization should loosen the leash occasionally so that the in-house designer can attend conferences and exhibitions to recharge. "Last spring, after visiting the Milan Furniture Fair, I was so excited that I felt fresh and motivated, as if it were my first days with the company again," says Helene Prablanc, Director of Product Design for Korres Natural Products in Greece.

- Adequate resources: this could include—but not be limited to—budget, hardware/software, employees, training, reference material, and office hardscape. But the designer's world sometimes requires more specialized tools that other departments may not require: more lighting, less lighting, more windows, less windows, a high table, flat files, plenty of fonts, and more. The designer may have

to justify such purchases, so be prepared to offer evidence of a return on investment.

Securing full value: the designer's role

- Communication is crucial. Its importance is two-fold: first, co-workers directly related to a project need to know what is going on. The second issue is one of perception. Since the design process can be somewhat invisible for long stretches, updates let those outside of the department know that you are working as hard as they are.

- Know as much as you can about your company and its business. Knowledge is definitely power in this arena. "If there is a designer who does not know the business inside and out, that person is playing with his career. You have to be proactive about becoming educated, not reactive," says Michele Floriani, Brand Manager for BMC Software.

1 Being involved from the very start of the project—as Art Director Guy Kelly was on this book—was key to its unique approach and success. He not only designed the book, he was also part of a group of editors and designers who selected the inside art.
Designer: Guy Kelly; artist: Aaron Westerberg

"I entered a PC world when I joined the team here, and our IT department was reluctant to see the light. After I had been on a PC for about eight months, our IT director went to a conference where someone told him I would be more productive on a Mac. That sold him. I was able to get the laptop of my choosing after that."

In-house designer for a national restaurant chain

1

■ In addition, in-house designers must understand the emotional and psychological needs of their clients. This knowledge comes from empathy and regular eyeball-to-eyeball contact, not data. The outward manifestation of this is behaving in a way that is appropriate to the organization. "Designers are often scrutinized as it is because of the stigma that we're jeans-wearing, Mac-loving hippies who don't know how to act in the business world," says Cindy Reynolds, a designer with Zaxby's Franchising, a company which franchises casual restaurants. "But we do know how to act. Treat the people you're designing for as if they were an outside client, because they are the reason why you have a job in the first place."

■ Be extremely organized. Keep excellent records. Be flexible and patient.

■ Respect the schedule, without fail. Constantly update and maintain a calendar that everyone can easily reference. Give honest predictions of how long things will take and give frequent updates.

■ Be strategic: look at your own department as a business. Be smart about the projects you pursue. Write down every project that is in motion, from cocktail napkins to enormous promotional

❶ Sometimes getting the right resources is just a matter of asking. When Zaxby's Franchising designer Cindy Reynolds found herself assigned the job of photographer for a professional golfer her company was sponsoring, her first day's shoot did not go well due to the lack of a zoom lens. She returned to the office, made her plea, and within an hour, had the lens.

campaigns. Which projects can you do well? Which projects might be best handled outside?

- Offer training so that others understand design better. Also consider incentives to those who partner well with you. For instance, offer discounts for early requests. Or, when a department has given design sufficient time to do good work and the finished product reflects this, turn those projects into "good example" case studies and share them with the rest of the organization. Let high-level managers know which departments are partnering with you best.

- Remember why you are there. It is crucial to think the same way an independent design firm does: is the work achieving what the company needs? If not, the outside firm will lose the client. The in-house designer won't lose the client; he will lose his job. Also, in the coldest possible terms, an in-house design group is generally an overhead, not a profit center. So it's wise to not let complacency sneak in.

- Maintain a customer service attitude. Meet all deadlines—in fact, meet all promises. "The amount of pressure we are under is due to the amount of pressure

❷ When you work with non-designers, it helps to use the same visual language that they do. Michele Floriani, Director of Branding and Creative Services for BMC Software, developed this simple chart that clearly explains to non-creatives the resources that design requires.

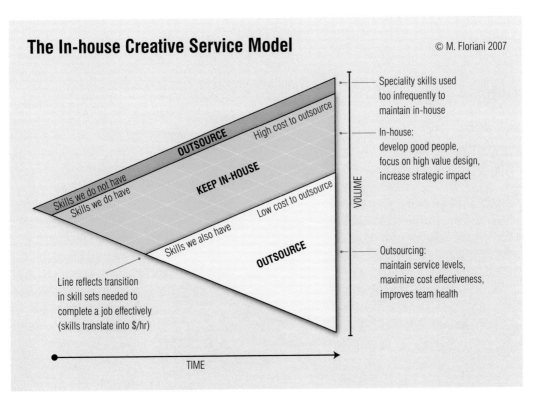

The In-house Creative Service Model

© M. Floriani 2007

Speciality skills used too infrequently to maintain in-house

In-house: develop good people, focus on high value design, increase strategic impact

Outsourcing: maintain service levels, maximize cost effectiveness, improves team health

OUTSOURCE   High cost to outsource
KEEP IN-HOUSE
Skills we do not have
Skills we do have
Low cost to outsource
Skills we also have
OUTSOURCE
VOLUME
TIME

Line reflects transition in skill sets needed to complete a job effectively (skills translate into $/hr)

①-③ Fashion house Oilily, with offices in the US and the Netherlands, has a very distinct look to its promotional pieces. Its in-house designers are best able to play their graphics off of various seasons' collections.

1 and 2: design/illustration: Sharon Coon
3: layout by Sharon Coon; photography: Oilily NL

1

2

our client is under," says Nina Kulhawy, Senior Designer with the Provost Communications Group at Arizona State University. "Knowing this puts me in their shoes, and I become more understanding."

- Those jobs that can be done quickly should be done quickly. Of course, no one likes to be interrupted in their regular stream of work, but if it's possible to show an extra degree of responsiveness, do it. But don't turn into a martyr or miracle worker—more on that later.

- Do what the client asks. It may not result in the most ambitious or creative solution, but it is important that the client is satisfied.

Develop a proactive process

- Develop simple forms that gather the right kind of information. Erin Smithmier of Helzberg Diamonds says that her organization uses a form called a Creative Job Start, which is saved on the network drive and also emailed to all internal clients who request design work. The form cannot be turned in without all of the necessary fields filled in—target audience, print process, sizing, necessary inclusions, final product output information, budget, goals, and more—so in effect, basic electronics ensure

that all necessary information is submitted before the project begins.

- The ideal routing of such a form prior to reaching the designer's desk would be:

1 It is submitted through the head of the requesting outside department (to keep him or her in the loop but also to prevent requests for personal Christmas cards or softball team T-shirts from plaguing you).
2 The form is delivered to the design department director or traffic manager, or, if no such personnel are in place, directly to the designer.
3 The designer who will be handling the project gives immediate feedback to the client regarding the information on the form and asking more questions.

- Face-to-face time is crucial after the form is received, something a form can't replace. Ask questions—lots of them. Ask until you run out of questions. The client may ask for a four-page brochure and will indicate that she will deliver the content to you via email. But what is that content? Text that may need to be formatted? A chart that needs to be completely reworked? Extremely low-res and therefore unprintable photos? For a web graphic, is it static? Animated? Why?

1 In-house designers not only follow brand standards more adeptly, they can also stray from them occasionally and still produce effective work. For a summer point-of-purchase series, designer Erin Smithmier and her team at Helzberg Diamonds safely stretched the brand standards.
Designer: Erin Smithmier; CD: Tracie Charvat; photographer: Hollis Officer

CaseStudy: *Heavy Hitter Project*

February 2007

PROJECT: Heavy Hitter Campaign
CLIENT: Cargo Marketing
CONTACT: Shelly Neal
DESIGNER: Sonia Avila

Objective: To educate and raise awareness of the increased weight limits in Cargo. In turn, this will enhance what our Customers can send and add to our bottomline.

Collateral: Pieces include a poster, dustcover, electronic art for web, and directmail (postcard).

Creative Challenges: To create something fresh for Cargo that draws the viewer in.

The Process: After initially meeting with Shelly and Dave, the Graphic

Design & Creative Services Team brainstormed various concepts. Initially we presented 8 taglines before landing on the "Heavy Hitter" concept. Then came the challenge of merging thoughts with the visual. We wanted a concept that really focused on how great this is for our Cargo Customers. Knowing that the Cargo Marketing Team wanted to make a bold splash, I knew the image needed to pack a punch. Through the use of very strong, weighty type and a bold color palette, the visual communication was both pleasing and informative.

Did the Solution Work?: "Yes. The piece captures exactly what we want to say with a graphic that is fun and unexpected for Cargo."—Shelly Neal

For more information, contact Cargo Marketing or swacargo.com

INTRODUCING
A **NEW HEAVY HITTER**
NEW WEIGHT LIMIT
200 lbs. per piece
SEAFOOD WEIGHT LIMIT
175 lbs. per piece
SOUTHWEST CARGO

① & ② The graphic design group at Southwest Airlines sends out monthly Quick Tips or Creative Case Studies to clients throughout the company. These missives provide design basics in layman's terms. "We do this because we were having problems with

CaseStudy: *Dress Code Project*

April 2007

PROJECT: Dress Code Posters
CLIENT: Employee Communications
CONTACT: Katie Coldwell
DESIGNER: Quyen Dong

Objective: To raise awareness of the Company's dress code.

Collateral: Posters

Creative Challenges: To design the message in a eye-catching and effective manner by balancing the right mix of humor while being aware of Employees' sensitivities.

The Process: The Employee Communications Team came to me with the idea of creating Dress

Code Posters with a little bit of an edge. Initially, characters for the poster were discussed, and off I went to conceptualize their traits, while maintaining our Southwest wit. I then placed speech bubbles strategically to draw the viewers attention to certain problematic areas. After presenting my first draft to the Employee Communications Team, they took the design, and came back to me with changes, and verbiage for the posters. Originally, Dirty Dan and Inappropriate Izzy were horrendous. Let's just say they had flies, fungus, and fuzz. After putting the final touches to the posters, they were printed and distributed.

Did the Solution Work?: "The posters created for us by the GD&CS Team were the perfect embodiment of information, tact, and humor."—Katie Coldwell

For more information, contact Employee Communications

CaseStudy: *NYSE Invitation*

June 2007

PROJECT: NYSE Investors Invitation
CLIENT: Finance
CONTACT: Ryan Martinez and Tony Rodriguez
DESIGNER: John Jones

Objective: To invite Stockholders to the Opening Bell of the NYSE and subsequent meeting.

Collateral: Invitations

Creative Challenges: To design an invitation that combined a Southwest sense of humor with an expensive look.

The Process: Investor Relations wanted an invitation that had a

similar look to a piece that our Team had produced previously. I used some of the charts from that project, and came up with verbiage that complimented the look of the invitation. I wanted to keep it very simple and concise. In order to create a more elegant look, I went with a metallic ink with an aqueous coating to prevent the ink from smudging (metallic inks tend to rest on the top of the paper, and are more likely to rub off or show fingerprints). After the approval process and a few revisions, the invitation and matching envelopes were printed by Newman Graphics.

clients making errors when sending us files, such as low-res photos for print publications, or just not understanding the design process," says John Jones, graphic design specialist for Southwest Airlines.

Sonia Avila, Quyen Dong, Trent Duran, John Jones

Quick Tip: *Type 101*

January 2007

Type creates an instant emotion. Its shape and placement communicate as quickly as an image but do you know the differences that make type unique? Here is the 101 on type.

To begin let's start with the challenge of **font** versus **typeface**. How often have we heard someone refer to letters on a screen or on paper a font? People often confuse the terms and simple refer to every letter form as a font. But unfortunately what you see is not a font. Here's the breakdown…

A **typeface** is the design of the alphabet. The letters, numbers, and symbols are type.

Arial, Times New Roman, Cooper Black, and Bauer Bodoni (just two samples) are all typefaces.

Fonts are simply the digital files that contain the typefaces. These digital files are what printers use to transcribe the information and print the work.

Now that we now know the difference I am sure you are wondering why some type has serifs (the small strokes at the end of a letter) and others do not? **Serif** type contains small strokes (or "feet") at the end of the letter forms. Typefaces like Times New Roman are perfect examples of type containing serifs. Arial would be an example of a **sans serif** (san meaning "withough") type. Now feel free to type circles around your friends.

— Type:
Bauer Bodoni

— Type:
News Gothic
sans serif

Quick Tip: *Owning the Brand*

May 2007

Admit it, we've all been there … someone asks about that unique shade of blue on our planes. And more often than not, we all reply, "Oh that's Canyon Blue."

From Canyon Blue, to Plak (that ever present typeface on our billboards), to our Takeoff logo, these elements all combine to help shape Southwest's visual identity. Understanding the elements, how they work, and how they should be used is our responsibility as proud Employees. A strong brand not

only helps you gain an edge in recognition, but also makes the brand less dissolvable. The accompanying PDF contains a wealth of information. Here's a quick quiz to test your Takeoff logo knowledge.

Q: **Which of the following is correct?**

A: If you selected B, you're right. Logos A and C may appear correct, but you'll notice slight flaws. A is skewed, C has Southwest Airlines and not the proper "Southwest," and D has been created using a "watermark" effect with type obstructing the actual logo. If you are uncertain about usage of a particular logo or any other brand element, give us a call. Let's keep the Southwest brand strong!

A

SOUTHWEST

C

SOUTHWEST AIRLINES

B

SOUTHWEST

D

Southwest Airlines
Pogo Stick
Jumping Club
SOUTHWEST

Quick Tip: *Color Theory*

July 2007

As designers, our eyes glaze over with glee as we thumb through Pantone swatch books. We crave color and can quickly rattle off that Southwest's shade of red is Pantone 485. To help pass off our enthusiasm for color, we thought we'd share a few basics and trends.

Warm v. Cool Colors:
Warm colors are associated with daylight (red, orange, yellow) Cool colors are associated with overcast or gray days (blues, greens, violets)

Color Psychology:
• Blues and Greens are tranquil and calming
• Red stimulates the senses and can raise blood pressure
• Black is the color of authority and power
• White symbolizes innocence and purity
• Green is the most popular decorating color and symbolizes nature
• Yellow is optimistic
• Purple is the color of royalty, luxury, wealth, and sophistication
• Brown is reliable and the color of the earth

Current Hot Colors: Olive, Eggplant, Deep Red, Avocado, Espresso/Coffee Colors, Chocolate

The New Red: Orange. Unlike red, orange gives off a friendlier vibe.

2007 Color of the Year:
Chili Pepper Red

Designer's Picks:
Trent: Red
Quyen: Green
John: Green
Sonia: Red

TIPS FOR EFFECTIVE DESIGN

Michele Floriani, Director of Branding for BMC Software, developed this checklist which he and his 18-person in-house group uses to make certain that the work they are doing is completely effective.

- Are we providing agency-quality work at a discounted price?
- Are we more familiar with the topics/ products than outside resources?
- Are we moving faster because we have inside visibility?
- Are we extending our services into areas that would normally be cost-prohibitive to the company if done externally?
- Are we going farther because we have a vested interest in the success of all that is accomplished at BMC?

- The words "great design" and "committee decision" almost never go together. Work gets watered-down, compromised, twisted, reduced, and, in general, diminished. If committee rule is part of your lot, analyze the situation to discover where exactly the design begins to go south. Would having more refined sketches to hand help? Is there a lack of defined production specs? No copy written yet? Bring as many of these elements and more to the party. Even if your ideas aren't perfect, they will help shape the discussion—hopefully, in a more palatable direction.

- Establish a brand review group that meets regularly to review all creative or marketing pieces produced by the company. This is particularly useful if departments other than the graphic design group are "designing" materials. The group can accept or decline the work, or ask that the work be revised. In this way, the in-house designer is not the only one policing and protecting the brand.

- If you have the personnel resources, set up your department like that of an outside design firm, with an art director or creative director, designers, traffic manager, production person and, perhaps most important, a receptionist/gatekeeper who makes certain that work is funneled in properly.

1

- Have a timetable to which everyone can easily refer. This schedule should show all of the projects which are pending or moving through your office at any one time and be updated daily, if possible. In this way, everyone can see exactly where his or her project is in the process. Then decisions can be made about adjusting delivery dates, bringing in external help, and more. It will also gently train those who constantly abuse the system, asking you to perform miracle after miracle.

"It is only a miracle once," says Ken Bullock. "After that, then it becomes the everyday. You set a nasty precedent. Once you show you can push it, it becomes the norm." Bullock is not against helping people out when he can, but he believes in giving a

① When a group of designers and communicators at Arizona State University redesigned the school's website home page, they posted comps and solicited feedback from other departments, faculty, students, and staff. "Everyone could look at our progress," explains Nina Kulhawy, a Senior Designer with the Provost Communications Group at Arizona State University. "I was surprised at how many people tuned in. Their feedback did direct the process, and people were so happy to be included."
Design: Gary Campbell, Cindi Farmer, Scott Worthington, Nina Kulhawy, Kathy Marks, Anish Adalja, Cameron Scholtz, Safwat Saleem, William Atwood, Deborah Prewitt, Rex Clark, Natalie Goebig, Stacy Holmstedt, Adian Teo

① Listening was key to the success of this intriguing book cover, designed by Guy Kelly of F+W Publications. A compilation of many painting technique books, this manual was in production for two full years, with the input of many departments. The initial idea for the cover, in fact, came from a sales manager. "Despite what designers like to think, we're not the only ones with good ideas," Kelly says.

Art director: Guy Kelly; photographer: Al Parrish

modified "yes" when necessary. "If I don't deliver when I say, whether the schedule was ridiculous or not, it ruins my reputation, and it puts them in a deeper hole than they were already in. I am not serving anyone well."

■ Don't forget that design is a team effort, points out Bullock. "We have to have content, and the people who have that content is everybody else," he says.

■ Have a point person for each project, a single individual with whom you correspond.

■ When a project is complete, follow up with a quick (emailed) survey that asks the client about his experience and satisfaction. The resulting feedback can sometimes be painful/galling/tiresome, but real gifts will emerge from the dialog that will help improve the entire process.

"Under-promise and over-deliver."
Ken Bullock

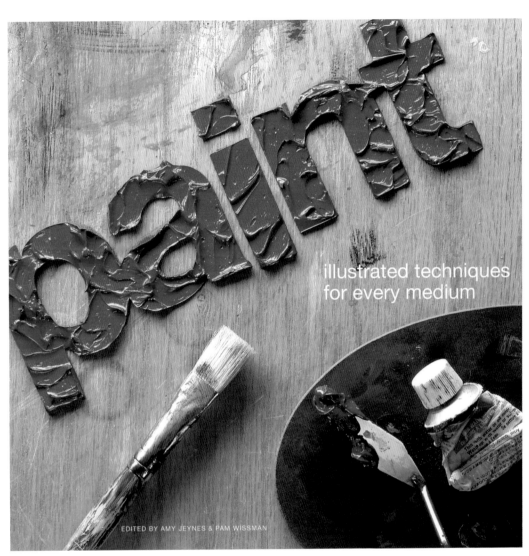

paint

illustrated techniques
for every medium

EDITED BY AMY JEYNES & PAM WISSMAN

Selling Your Ideas Up the Ladder

Kurt's desk had been his home away from home for the past two weeks. He had spent so much time there, working endlessly on the new website, that he and the cleaning guy had actually shared several Chinese take-out meals together. But he knew that at the presentation tomorrow, it would all be worth it.

Before he began proofreading the last few pages, Kurt flipped through his email. Instantly, his eyes caught a message from his boss, titled "Changes." His heart sank.

"In the site's section on the product features, could you drop in these new photos? I know that sales will bite on these. Thanks! See you in the morning."

Kurt looked at the attachment list: there were at least 20 new shots. He felt sick. The original set of photos had come directly from sales. Now what was he supposed to do? No matter what he did, someone was going to be unhappy.

Closing the deal

A designer can put her heart and soul into a project, but if the sale is not made at presentation time—for whatever reason—all that effort is for nothing. How can the chances for a successful sale be increased?

Pure and simple, you have to remember the core commercial reason you are there. You have to have a good understanding of where the company is going and prove that what you are presenting will support those values.

With the proper legwork done ahead of time, the sale should almost be at least 95 percent made by the time you walk in the conference room door. As discussed in the previous chapter, asking the right questions beforehand helps to make the sale later. These questions emerge from proper research done ahead of time and never from assumptions. The proposed design or presentation should reflect those answers directly: in fact, it doesn't hurt to have those complete surveys or the creative brief in hand so that you have physical proof of how their wishes were addressed.

In larger organizations, particularly, it is crucial to find like-minded people within the organization beforehand who "get" design and marketing. Make friends with these people right away, and maintain an ongoing dialog: they could emerge as your champions when most needed. Develop a consistent message and back each other up. When managers start hearing the same message from multiple sources, they are more willing to explore new ways of doing things.

Even better is an "angel" in the form of a chief financial officer or another company officer who is interested in and is willing to champion your cause. Secure this person's trust and keep him or her in the loop, no matter what.

However hard the designer tries to please, it's impossible to eliminate every jagged scrap of politics within an organization. To protect yourself from getting caught in the middle of a preexisting fight, insist on one contact from each outside department for each project, and make sure that person is in the room when the presentation is made. If having two or more "bosses" is unavoidable, try to sit

"The first realization for a designer who is trying to sell his services is to accept that everyone has an agenda which is to accomplish their own personal success. It's your job to identify what those agendas are and learn how to capitalize on them to facilitate buy-in. You, as a designer, must become in-tune with your own vision and strategize its alignment with that of other vested parties."

Nicole Roberts, Designer, Cooper Carry, architects

down with them prior to the presentation and address their concerns privately.

It's very important to have the right decision-makers in the room when the presentation is made. Learn the personal preferences of the leaders and the preferences of the corporate structure. Face-to-face time simply cannot be replaced by email or telephone. Whenever possible, the designers who created the work should present it: they have the most in-depth knowledge of and enthusiasm for the project.

❶ The Caribbean Studies Center at Casa de las Américas, where Pepe Menendez serves as Design Director, needed a visual identity for an event that would feature literature, painting, and music. The main concern was to avoid Caribbean clichés such as palm trees, dancing women, and sunsets. Menendez's solution was a hand made of waves, a human connection to the geography. It was so well received that the design became the group's logo.

1

"The very worst thing is the vice president who does not respect the brand and who has a secretary who is producing materials on the side."

Brand manager for a large software company

"I'm not comfortable speaking in front of a group," is not a valid excuse for shirking this crucial step in the creative process. Get comfortable. Practice, take classes on presenting, or ask a more accomplished speaker within your organization to coach you. Sitting mutely in a meeting simply reinforces the stereotype that designers aren't good businesspeople—and therefore don't need to be taken seriously.

No matter what you are presenting to a client, it is crucial to go at the proper speed. "Think evolution, not revolution," says Mary Ridgway, Art Director for University Relations at Fort Hays State University. Don't make huge jumps in logic or make surprise shifts in direction at presentation time. The client's confidence in your decisions needs

to have a safe amount of time and space in which to grow. "Over time, they are more willing to trust me and get a little more daring because I've demonstrated that I am in their corner."

When trying to sell a more experimental concept, something that might make management nervous, gather some numbers prior to the presentation—sales numbers of other similar products or direction whose design also takes some chances. Forget about trying to sell the visual/aesthetic part of the idea and focus on potential sales: after all, higher-ups who tend to be wary of anything new are usually nervous because they fear poor sales, not your design.

Also be conscious that while most people have a good degree of comfort with print, their knowledge of electronic designs is usually less. You may have created a cool Flash design, but your audience will compliment you on the great "video." You will have to include

❶ & ❷ Croatia Airlines has a distinct yet simple identity, created by Ivana Ivankovic Prilic and her team in the company's corporate design department. "The square," she says, "as a recognizable symbol of Croatian national identity, is placed in a dynamic form, representing movement or travel." The graphics are easily translateable between aircraft and other designs, such as print pieces.
*Annual report and magazine: Nenad Vujo_evi_*

1

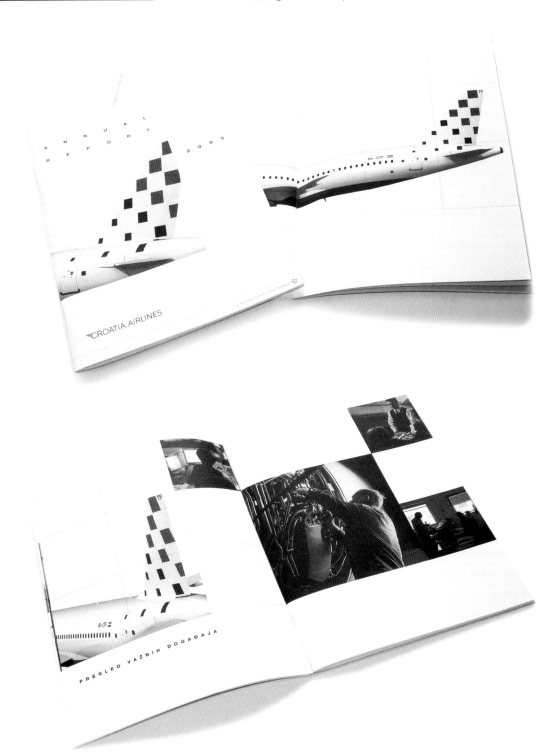

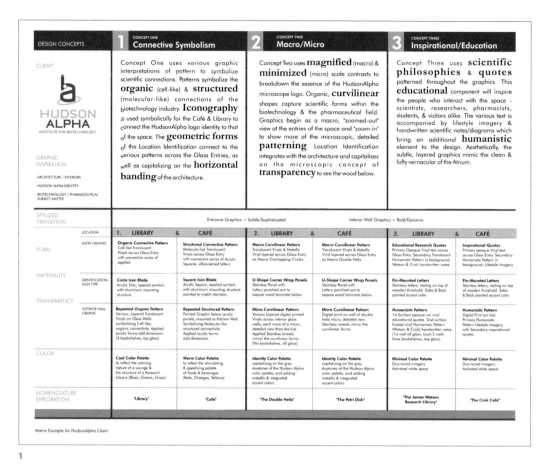

DESIGN CONCEPTS

1 — CONCEPT ONE — Connective Symbolism

Concept One uses various graphic interpretations of pattern to symbolize scientific connections. Patterns symbolize the **organic** (cell-like) & **structured** (molecular-like) connections of the biotechnology industry. **Iconography** is used symbolically for the Café & Library to connect the HudsonAlpha logo identity to that of the space. The **geometric forms** of the Location Identification connect to the various patterns across the Glass Entries, as well as capitalizing on the **horizontal banding** of the architecture.

2 — CONCEPT TWO — Macro/Micro

Concept Two uses **magnified** (macro) & **minimized** (micro) scale contrasts to breakdown the essence of the HudsonAlpha microscope logo. Organic, **curvilinear** shapes capture scientific forms within the biotechnology & the pharmaceutical field. Graphics begin as a macro, "zoomed-out" view at the entries of the space and "zoom-in" to show more of the microscopic, detailed **patterning**. Location Identification integrates with the architecture and capitalizes on the microscopic concept of **transparency** to see the wood below.

3 — CONCEPT THREE — Inspirational/Education

Concept Three uses **scientific philosophies** & **quotes** patterned throughout the graphics. This **educational** component will inspire the people who interact with the space - scientists, researchers, pharmacists, students, & visitors alike. The various text is accompanied by lifestyle imagery & handwritten scientific notes/diagrams which bring an additional **humanistic** element to the design. Aesthetically, the subtle, layered graphics mimic the clean & lofty vernacular of the Atrium.

CLIENT: HUDSON ALPHA — INSTITUTE FOR BIOTECHNOLOGY

GRAPHIC INSPIRATION:
- ARCHITECTURE / INTERIORS
- HUDSON ALPHA IDENTITY
- BIOTECHNOLOGY / PHARMACEUTICAL SUBJECT MATTER

STYLIZED TRANSITION: Entrance Graphics = Subtle/Sophisticated — Interior Wall Graphics = Bold/Dynamic

LOCATION	1. LIBRARY	CAFÉ	2. LIBRARY	CAFÉ	3. LIBRARY	CAFÉ
FORM — ENTRY GRAPHIC	**Organic Connective Pattern** Cell-like Translucent Vinyls across Glass Entry with connective series of Acrylic applied	**Structured Connective Pattern** Molecule-like Translucent Vinyls across Glass Entry with connective series of Acrylic Squares, silkscreened letters	**Macro Curvilinear Pattern** Translucent Vinyls & Metallic Vinyl layered across Glass Entry as Macro Overlapping Circles.	**Macro Curvilinear Pattern** Translucent Vinyls & Metallic Vinyl layered across Glass Entry as Macro Double Helix.	**Educational Research Quotes** Primary Opaque Vinyl text across Glass Entry. Secondary Translucent Humanistic Pattern in background, Watson & Crick handwritten notes.	**Inspirational Quotes** Primary opaque Vinyl text across Glass Entry. Secondary Humanistic Pattern in background, Lifestyle imagery.
MATERIALITY — IDENTIFICATION SIGN TYPE	**Circle Icon Blade** Acrylic Disc, applied symbol, with aluminum mounting structure	**Square Icon Blade** Acrylic Square, applied symbol, with aluminum mounting structure painted to match stainless	**U-Shape Corner Wrap Panels** Stainless Panel with Letters punched-out to expose wood laminate below	**U-Shape Corner Wrap Panels** Stainless Panel with Letters punched-out to expose wood laminate below	**Pin-Mounted Letters** Stainless letters, resting on top of wooden threshold. Sides & Back painted accent color	**Pin-Mounted Letters** Stainless letters, resting on top of wooden threshold. Sides & Back painted accent color
TRANSPARENCY — INTERIOR WALL GRAPHIC	**Repeated Organic Pattern** Various, Layered Translucent Vinyls on Glass Walls symbolizing Cell-like, organic connectivity. Applied acrylic forms add dimension. (3 bookshelves, top glass)	**Repeated Structured Pattern** Painted Graphic below acrylic panels, mounted to Kitchen Wall. Symbolizing Molecule-like structured connectivity. Applied acrylic forms add dimension.	**Micro Curvilinear Pattern** Various Layered digital printed Vinyls across interior glass walls, each more of a micro, detailed view than the last. Applied Stainless reveals mirror the curvilinear forms (No bookshelves, all glass)	**Micro Curvilinear Pattern** Digital print on wall of double helix micro, detailed view. Stainless reveals mirror the curvilinear forms	**Humanistic Pattern** 1st Surface opaque cut vinyl educational quotes. 2nd surface frosted vinyl Humanistic Pattern (Watson & Crick) handwritten notes. (1st wall all glass, back 2 walls have bookshelves, top glass)	**Humanistic Pattern** Digital Print (on tile) Primary Humanistic Pattern Lifestyle imagery, with Secondary inspirational quotes.
COLOR	**Cool Color Palette** to reflect the calming nature of a Lounge & the structure of a Research Library (Blues, Greens, Greys)	**Warm Color Palette** to reflect the stimulating & appetizing palette of foods & beverages (Reds, Oranges, Yellows)	**Identity Color Palette** capitalizing on the gray duotones of the Hudson Alpha color palette, and adding metallic & integrated accent colors.	**Identity Color Palette** capitalizing on the gray duotones of the Hudson Alpha color palette, and adding metallic & integrated accent colors.	**Minimal Color Palette** Duo-toned imagery Activated white space	**Minimal Color Palette** Duo-toned imagery Activated white space
NOMENCLATURE EXPLORATION	"Library"	"Café"	"The Double Helix"	"The Petri Dish"	"The James Watson Research Library"	"The Crick Café"

Matrix Example for HudsonAlpha Client

1

① The in-house environmental graphics studio at Cooper Carry Architects uses this matrix as an internal organizational tool. It documents the origin of the graphic designers' concepts, which helps keep project managers and the design team on track throughout the process. It explains how the design is directly connected to the company's architectural work and vision of their project, thereby improving understanding and buy-in from above. Lastly, the matrix keys into the current realities and potential opportunities for the project.

Designer: Nicole R. Roberts; principal architect: Mark Jensen, AIA, LEED; client: Hudson Alpha Institute for Biotechnology

"An editor and I came up with a very experimental idea that we loved. We took it to the committee, made a great presentation, and everyone there loved it. But that wasn't the final approval stage: it still had to be presented by someone else to management—and they shot it down really fast. They didn't have the benefit of our presentation or explanation. It was a reminder to maintain direct contact with the people who make the final decisions."

Guy Kelly, Designer, F+W Publications

TIPS FOR SELLING

How to improve your chances of making the sale, from Mary Ridgway, an in-house designer for nearly 30 years.

- Double-check that your proposal makes logical sense.
- Be organized.
- Be clean and concise.
- Don't play into the flaky artist stereotype.
- Emulate your clientele.
- Be respectful and appreciative of the mission of the organization.
- Show how your proposal fits the mission and purpose.
- Make allies whenever possible.
- Smile and be enthusiastic.
- No whining or excuses.
- Be realistic.
- Don't try to fake your way through something you don't really know.
- Get back to the client with information they request.
- Know how to write and spell correctly.

① A combination of stock and assigned photography helped form a set of effective solutions for Marshfield Clinics. The in-house designer knew that the organization's graphics needed to look stylish but could not be too expensive.
Design: Erik Borreson; photo: Liquid Library

"I have matured as a designer, overcoming the urge to dwell on the trials of the business. Before, I was overcome by the 'In-house Design Monster,' which slithers into your studio after you've returned from a bad client meeting and steals your passion for design."

Environmental graphic designer for a national corporation

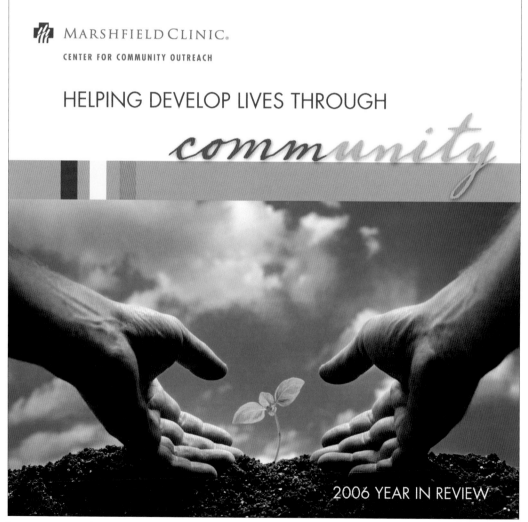

MARSHFIELD CLINIC.

CENTER FOR COMMUNITY OUTREACH

HELPING DEVELOP LIVES THROUGH

community

2006 YEAR IN REVIEW

1

in your presentation some explanation of how the digital design works, but don't blind them with science. Any new media increases the level of trepidation, and you don't want that to get in the way of your sale. You want to make them more comfortable, not less.

Sometimes the designer finds him- or herself working on a client-suggested idea that just feels wrong-headed. What then? "First do a proposal the way the client has asked for it, then offer a second mock-up using your idea," Mary Ridgway of Middlebury College suggests. "If your idea is good, it will shine brilliantly next to the original."

If a presentation incorporates ideas from a number of people, when the idea or comp is presented, it is half-sold already. Acknowledge valuable individual contributions, however small.

When your part of the presentation is made and the comments start to roll in—and this is the most painful, difficult thing at times—don't take it personally. This isn't an exhibit of personal work; it's your job. "It may be art, but then, not everyone even likes Picasso," says Cora Lanier of Shamir Insight. "You need to detach yourself. It's not your baby. It's just a piece of paper."

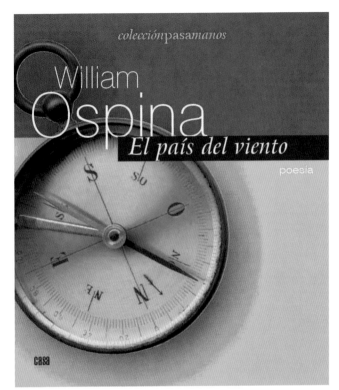

2

"We used to produce presentation boards like crazy. Now, we do slide presentations, show lots more visuals, and even include a soundtrack that gets people really excited. This kind of presentation sets a different tone—it's fun and exciting. But everything we do has to go back to the business objectives."

Joerg Metzner, Design Director, Rand McNally

❷ Casa de las Américas' Pasamanos Collection releases books infrequently, but the series still needed a consistent identity. Design Director Pepe Menendez developed an easily recognizable cover style: the page is split in two, and an object plays the main visual role, followed by the author's name and the book's title.

Creative Strategies

More than once in his career as an in-house designer, Nick had wished he had studied chess a little closer. He had no idea that being a designer would involve so much strategy, so much out-thinking. For the third consecutive year, he found himself making a presentation to an assorted assembly of doubtful-looking vice presidents, trying once again to convince them to outfit his entire department with Macs.

But this time would be different. Today, he knew he would win. His presentation was all about improved time efficiencies, streamlined production, and reduced printing costs. It was all numbers.

"So you're saying that just by changing platforms, you can save $15,000 per year in printing and take two days off of every run?" asked one skeptical VP, flipping through the charts Nick had painstakingly prepared.

"At least," the art director replied, as eyebrows raised and heads nodded all around the table.

The title of this chapter—Creative Strategies—can be read in two ways. In one context, it can be read as "strategies for being creative" with the resources that you have. In another, it can be understood as "strategies that *are* creative." For our purposes, both interpretations work equally well.

It's necessary for the in-house designer to always have a quiver full of strategies for being creative, and not only for designing. That's because, almost universally, resources are notoriously short for this tribe—budget, people, equipment, space, and (always) time. The strategies that are themselves creative have more to do with demonstrating value and return on investment, negotiating, and "committee-proofing" your work.

Budget management
Charge-backs

The budget management system most commonly associated with in-house design is charge-backs. Pure and simple, those in the company who use the in-house design department are charged for it, either in monies that are taken out of their budgets (usually invisibly, through the company's accounting system) or in hour units that are subtracted from allotments given to them. Charge-back systems are especially common in organizations in which there are many products or segments that need attention, such as a company that produces hundreds of different personal care products, for instance: the time allotted to each separate product can be tracked more accurately. The system is also used by organizations that are far-flung geographically, but whose disparate pieces all use the same in-house design group.

They are also common, however, in companies where the in-house design department needs the system in place to prevent abuse of their time—say, to keep those people away who just want you to whip up a T-shirt design for their daughter's soccer team or the salesperson who wants to get a brochure reworked for the umpteenth time. If there is no way to account on the spreadsheet for the time spent, then the designer can easily and guiltlessly say, "Sorry."

1 Advance Auto Part's Endurance brand packaging is printed in China through the combined coordination of the company's North American and Chinese design teams. "Working directly with our design counterpart in China helps us to manage time and budgets. It also gives us a designer on-site working directly with the printers to ensure quality standards," explains Senior Designer Anne Clayton.
Senior designer: Marcie Phoebus; creative director: Shawn Murray; production designer: Danny So; printer/manufacturer: Li & Fung

1

"I'm not really fond of charge-backs. But a controlled way of doing a charge-back is to create a checks-and-balances system for which we make a ledger—a giant checkbook, really—and anything related to that project gets entered into the ledger, so we always know how much we have 'spent.'"

Chuck Kijak, Manager of Creative Services for Crayola

Charge-backs are also handy to spotlight the value of the in-house team and/or the organization's misuse of that value.

"I don't have a charge-back system, but I operate and manage my department as if I do," explains Glenn John Arnowitz, Director of Corporate Graphics for Wyeth. "There are charges associated with everything my department does, along with an hourly rate, and these are captured in an online project management system that provides reporting functionality, historical data, and shows the cost-savings of in-sourcing compared to out-sourcing."

Arnowitz also points out that a charge-back system—even an unofficial one to which only the design team is privy—can help an in-house designer identify "low-value" projects and projects the client could do without: over time, it should be easy to demonstrate to management where ROI is poor. As such projects are eliminated, the designer should be afforded more time to devote to high-value projects. The system also highlights when unnecessary revisions and reprints are being requested due to client error—for instance, because of careless proofreading before a job went to press.

Become part of the process

Charge-backs may have their uses. But of the hundreds of designers interviewed for this book, not one was an energetic advocate of the system. Two reasons prevail: first, it takes time to comply with the system (which is usually imposed by the organization, not the design group), even if a department is using software that helps to track time. That's time that could be better spent on design. Second, all of those neatly stacked hourly units are then up for the scrutiny of higher-ups who may or may not agree that the designer is spending his time wisely.

Far better, say most, is for the designer to be able to determine the proper amount of time a project takes and be able to say if it does

①-② Constituents of the Lance Armstrong Foundation expect—because of identity history and cost-efficiencies that all not-for-profits are expected to practice—designs that are yellow or yellow and black. For the foundation's versatile in-house design group, this is not at all a limitation.
Art director: Diana Berno; designers: Matthew Bromley, Tom Berno; printer: The Lithoprint Company; photography: Matt Lankes, Kreutz Photography

1

THE MANIFESTO OF THE LANCE ARM...

We believe in life.
Your life.
We believe in living every minute of it...
And that you must not let cancer take...
We believe in energy: channeled and...
We believe in focus: getting smart an...
Unity is strength. Knowledge is power...
This is the Lance Armstrong Founda...

We kick in the moment you're diagno...
We help you accept the tears. Acknow...
We believe in your right to live witho...
We believe in information. Not pity.
And in straight, open talk about can...
With husbands, wives and partners. W...
And the people you live with, work w...
This is no time to pull punches.
You're in the fight of your life.

We're about the hard stuff.
Like finding the nerve to ask for a sec...
And a third, or a fourth, if that's who...
We're about getting smart about all...
And if it comes to it, being in contr...
It's your life. You will have it your ...

We're about the practical stuff.
Planning for surviving. Banking y...
Organizing your finances. Dealin...
Insurance companies and employ...
It's knowing your rights.
It's your life.
Take no prisoners.

We're about the fight.
We're your champion on Capitol H...
healthcare system. Your sponsor...
And we know the fight never end...
Cancer may leave your body, but...
This is the Lance Armstrong Fou...
Founded and inspired by one of t...
cancer survivors on the planet.

LIVESTRONG

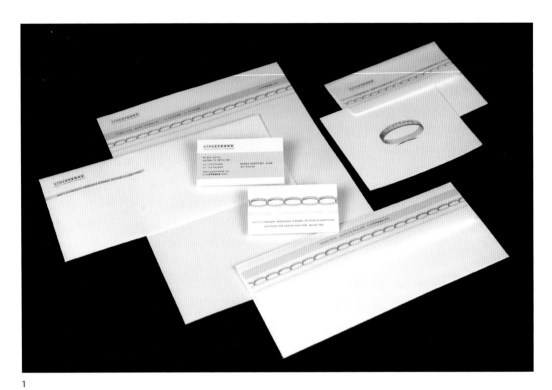

1

2

3

1-**4** More examples of the distinctive yellow-and-black designs from the Lance Armstrong Foundation.
Art director: Diana Berno; designers: Matthew Bromley, Tom Berno; printer: The Lithoprint Company; photography: Matt Lankes, Kreutz Photography

or does not work into a schedule already in motion. Each project gets the appropriate amount of attention as deemed by the expert—the designer.

Keeping the soccer team mom at bay can be handled in other ways— a departmental policy issued by a local vice president, for example, or by a traffic manager who intercepts at the door every job coming into the department.

The situation Jane Scherbaum faces as manager of the design department of the Victoria & Albert Museum is likely very common: sometimes her staff determines the budget within their group, and sometimes they are simply given a budget. But being handed a budget does not mean that the designer can have no influence in the allotment. "The most important thing if you are not in control of determining the budget is to try to get involved with advising the

person who does set it," she says. "In that way, even if we are given a budget, we can say straightaway if it is not enough. Or, if the budget is small, we will tell them it will limit what we can do. Sometimes, it's frustrating and we have to work inside of what we are given. But sometimes, another £1,000 will appear."

Having a seat at budget meetings or at least earning an advisory role can be to the great benefit of the

4

"We often try to present a 'shoot for the moon' option versus a standard quality one. If the client is sold on the 'big' design one, budget can be reallocated to produce it. We have to advocate strongly for designs that we feel are different/special/unique, while staying true to brand standards."

Fanny Lau, Designer, publications and internal marketing,

Museum of Science, Boston

larger organization: early in the process, the designer can suggest alternative solutions that make smarter use of the available money. He or she also has the budget-stretching supplier contacts that others in the company don't. "Be completely open with your suppliers—tell them what budget you have. Let them tell you what they can do for you. We get the maximum value by getting quotes from three to four sources and by building relationships with our sources," Scherbaum says.

Another huge advantage of including the design department in the budgeting process is the designer's ability to reallocate monies on the fly when necessary, says Senk Aljosa, designer with the retailer Merkur, in Slovenia. The response time of consumers is much quicker today, he says, and design and marketing are especially in tune with these movements. "Because we are reviewing the entire [marketing] process, we are increasing our agility and can cut costs, which are reallocated to the development stage or some other

conceptual stage that will have a decisive influence on the competitive advantage later on," Aljosa points out.

What will it cost?
It's the ever-present question. Ideally, the cost should be as small as possible for the best possible results: that outcome benefits everyone (and is so dissimilar to the cost mounted by an outside group, which needs to recover costs plus gain a profit). So to be considered as a serious partner in the budgeting process, the designer must prove that he or she can actually effect positive change. The clearest way to do this is to demonstrate constant, conscientious policing of client budgets. New and different ways to save must constantly be brought forward.

John Cianti, director of the in-house design group for Harman Consumer Group, is constantly looking for ways to gang printing, use alternate papers, and new printing techniques. "We have two high-end, high-capacity Canon Imagepress color copiers. For short runs of in-house material, these are excellent. We can print for pennies," Cianti reports. "We also have an in-house digital photo studio. We have negotiated a very good day-rate with a photographer. He uses our equipment and studio, saving many thousands of dollars over an outside photographer. Most of our budget activities involve protecting the budget of our clients."

Time management

When it comes to time and in-house design, there are three certainties:

1 There is never enough time.
2 There needs to be a definite schedule.
3 The schedule will change at a moment's notice.

There's not too much to be done about the first dilemma: it seems that no matter how much time is built into a schedule, it's never sufficient. So it's more a matter of how to spend that time effectively. "I've NEVER been given ample time to develop a well-thought-out campaign," says one harried designer who works for a large North American manufacturer. She has a sage solution. "Spend more time on the concept, the idea, and the message. If you've got that right, the rest goes quickly."

As any experienced in-house designer can report, it's impossible to set pre-fab time frames for certain sorts of projects: a brochure takes this long, while a logo takes that long, for example. It just doesn't work that way. But it is possible to use prior project schedules as a guide and, with the help of the client, to determine how long a specific project might take and make the client responsible for his part in preserving that schedule.

1 Don Twerdun, Creative Director for The Co-operators, an Ontario-based insurance and investment company, sometimes uses company employees as models in his designs, as he did for this corporate publication. It does sometimes save money, but he also feels it builds a better emotional connection with readers (other employees and agents) and it builds pride. *Creative director: Don Twerdun; senior designer: Brenda McKinney; photographer: Brad Scott*

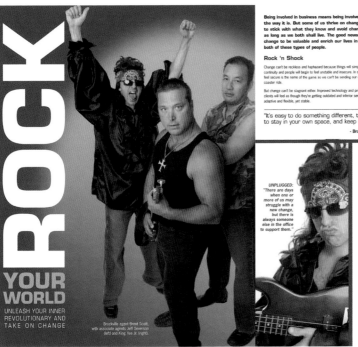

Brockville agent Brent Scott, with associate agents Jeff Severson (left) and King Yen Jr. (right).

ROCK YOUR WORLD
UNLEASH YOUR INNER REVOLUTIONARY AND TAKE ON CHANGE

Being involved in business means being involved in change. It's just the way it is. But some of us thrive on change while others want to stick with what they know and avoid change forever and ever as long as we both shall live. The good news is that in order for change to be valuable and enrich our lives in some way, we need both of these types of people.

Rock 'n Shock

Change can't be reckless and haphazard because things will simply fall apart. There will be no continuity and people will begin to feel unstable and insecure. In our business, making people feel secure is the name of the game so we can't be sending our clients on a daily roller coaster ride.

But change can't be stagnant either. Improved technology and processes will pass us by and clients will feel as though they're getting outdated and inferior service. Companies need to be adaptive and flexible, yet stable.

"It's easy to do something different, the challenge is to stay in your own space, and keep it good."
- Brad Whitford, Aerosmith

UNPLUGGED: "There are days when one or more of us may struggle with a new change, but there is always someone else in the office to support them."

"As the present now will later be past, the order is rapidly fading. And the first one now will later be last, for the times they are a-changin'."
- Bob Dylan

Taking Care of Business

When it comes to something like Client Relationship Management (CRM), we needed to look at what will benefit through change, as well as what has to stay the same. "CRM won't change our mission, goals or values, or the fundamental principles of running a sound financial services company," says Rick, Sr. VP of Direct Distribution. "But it will impact the way we deliver products and services to customers on a day-to-day basis. It's an opportunity to reinvent the way we do business."

What it comes down to is the reason we're here – our clients. So changing to a CRM philosophy makes sense because it puts our clients at the centre of all that we do, while our vision and values remain unwavering. In fact, CRM builds upon them.

So let's say a new concept, process, or program has been carefully evaluated and it's been determined that implementing it will be a beneficial and positive change. Customers will be happier, employees will be more efficient, and all will be right with the world. But even the best change is still change – we still have to do something different from what we're used to. So how do we adapt to change?

To change or not to change? Proof that everything needs to be judged on its own merits:
"We don't like their sound. Groups of guitars are on the way out."
- Decca Records rejecting The Beatles in 1962

6

1

1 & **2** Hiring an outside photographer to shoot product shots in their own digital photo studio and ganging projects on press are only two ways that the in-house design team at Harman, a leading audio/visual equipment manufacturer, saves money. Sample pages from the group's award-winning 2006 catalog are shown. *Director: John Cianti; art directors: Bob Abbatecola, Mike Keeley; photos: Russ Pratt; copy: Bill Kurth*

Life is a road trip. **Loud** is good, but **clear** is better. Can we please keep **driving** until this song is over? Have we got enough gas? Have we got enough **bass**? Born to be **wild**. Sorry, Officer, my mind was **somewhere** else.

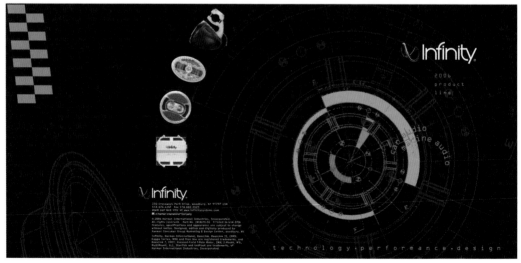

- PROPRIETARY
  STAMPED-STEEL
  BASKET

- PROGRESSIVE
  SPIDER

- VENTED POLEPIECE,
  NEODYMIUM MOTOR

- IMPEDANCE
  SELECTOR

- WOVEN-GLASS-FIBER
  WOOFER CONE

kappa 102.7w

10" Selectable Impedance Subwoofer
Power handling RMS: 350 watts
Power handling Peak: 1400 watts
Sensitivity: 89dB
Frequency response: 25Hz – 400Hz
1- or 4-Ohm selectable
Woven-glass-fiber woofer cone
Neodymium motor
Vented polepiece
Mounting depth: 4-3/4"

kappa 104.7w

10" Selectable Impedance Subwoofer
Power handling RMS: 350 watts
Power handling Peak: 1400 watts
Sensitivity: 87dB
Frequency response: 25Hz – 400Hz
2- or 8-Ohm selectable
Woven-glass-fiber woofer cone
Neodymium motor
Vented polepiece
Mounting depth: 4-3/4"

kappa 122.7w

12" Selectable Impedance Subwoofer
Power handling RMS: 350 watts
Power handling Peak: 1400 watts
Sensitivity: 92dB
Frequency response: 23Hz – 400Hz
1- or 4-Ohm selectable
Woven-glass-fiber woofer cone
Neodymium motor
Vented polepiece
Mounting depth: 5"

kappa 124.7w

12" Selectable Impedance Subwoofer
Power handling RMS: 350 watts
Power handling Peak: 1400 watts
Sensitivity: 90dB
Frequency response: 23Hz – 400Hz
2- or 8-Ohm selectable
Woven-glass-fiber woofer cone
Neodymium motor
Vented polepiece
Mounting depth: 5"

kappa subwoofers

---

basslink® II and basslink 4sc

- BassLink® II is new from the ground up and incorporates progressive features and technology. First you will notice that the grilles covering the 10" subwoofer and 10" passive radiator are square. That's because the subwoofer and radiator are square. Infinity's goal was to maximize cone area to extract every last ounce of bass out of the modestly sized housing. This approach allowed us to do so. The BassLink II is also powered by the same great 250-watt Class D power amp found in our BassLink T. In addition to a full set of controls and superior adjustability, BassLink II is easily expanded using our all-new BassLink 4sc. This multiple-channel amplifier allows BassLink II to become the amplifier source for the entire vehicle, not just the bass. The BassLink 4sc also features a phantom center channel with a four-position image control, allowing you to really dial your system in.

- BassLink 4sc. Multichannel amplifier expansion module for BassLink II. 50 Watts x 4 amplifier. Phantom center channel, front and rear level controls. Four-position phantom center control.

2005

> **"Clients are part of the process, and they can destroy the production schedule faster than anyone. I make it clear to them that they are part of the process, and if they don't do as planned, I can't help them meet their goals."**
>
> *Mary Ridgeway, Art Director, Fort Hayes State University*

(It should be noted here that there are plenty of project- and time-management software products available today. Some are quite sophisticated and can yield amazing results relating to output and billing. But each system requires a human administrator, so we will focus here on the human role rather than on technology.)

At the start of a project, a quick meeting with the client and the completion of a thorough project brief will establish the job's parameters. The agreed-upon schedule can be on paper or on screen, but it should be something that actually can be distributed to and signed by those involved in the process, both at the time of its creation and as the project proceeds. A handshake and a verbal agreement won't do.

Some in-house groups post their schedules so that they are visible to anyone—at the entrance to the department, outside of each designer's office, or on an intranet accessible to anyone in the organization. Such postings are a clear and constant visual reminder that A) the schedule is already tight, B) there are other projects ahead of yours, and C) if you step out of line, you will almost certainly lose your place.

Once the schedule is determined, the designer must accept—however discomforting it might be—that it is not carved in stone. It must be reevaluated constantly and adjusted as necessary. Juggling is inevitable—so much so, in fact, that many art directors interviewed for this book indicated that the ability to be flexible and cheerfully juggle projects when needed was a key attribute they looked for in new employees.

Still, the "open schedule" must be monitored, either by the designer or by project/traffic managers. Monthly, weekly, daily, even hourly reviews are necessary. What is a priority first thing in the morning may be demoted by lunch by an even more pressing project. "Every morning I look over my jobs in progress to assess the urgency among them and the complexity of the work involved in each," says Ceinwen Berrisford, until very recently an in-house designer with an Australian winery.

> **"Having a project manager who has a designer's mind is a good thing. There's better empathy and understanding there for what the design team is facing."**
>
> *Chuck Kijak, Manager of Creative Services for Crayola*

All this accommodation and flexibility does not mean, though, that the hapless designer should allow him- or herself to be buffeted about by everyone else's whims. The client can be held very accountable in the process.

Jane Scherbaum, design department manager of the Victoria & Albert Museum, has a very simple system that is lethally effective. "If [a client] misses a deadline by a week, say, without an explanation, we tell them that we have now readjusted the schedule and that the due date has been moved back a week as well. That way, they feel the impact of the delay," she explains, adding, "If they do call in advance to explain, I can be flexible."

Designers need to build up a certain resiliency or method that will enable them to put their collective foot down—to tell clients that a certain schedule has been adjusted to their detriment, that a deadline has become impossible, or that all jobs must be routed through a project or traffic manager. "It's a two-way thing," Scherbaum explains. "We are looking outward to our clients to make sure they use us in the best way. But at the same time, you have to look inward and make sure you are able to do the best you possibly can."

1 Partnering with executives means operating in an impeccably business-like manner. Jessica Espinel-Merte, a designer with Pitney Bowes, keeps a very exact record in a notebook of all jobs she has completed. All resources associated with projects, like those used for this project, are also filed exactly for quick retrieval.
Photos and design: Jessica Espinel-Merete

1

❶ & ❷ The Co-operators' design team hired less-experienced models and a friend for the photographs in these striking adverts, which preserved budget. "We took extra time in making everyone feel relaxed and didn't rush the shoot," says Creative Director Don Twerdun.

Creative director: Don Twerdun; designer: Jason Smith; photographer: Michael Davidson

Case Study   Tyndale House Publishers
Making Time

Todd Watkins is Design Manager for Tyndale House Publishers, a Christian book publisher based in the western suburbs of Chicago, which specializes in fiction, non-fiction, and the New Living Translation Bible. His group of 20 designers handles all of the book design and a majority of the marketing communication design for nearly 300 titles each year. His is a busy office. But he firmly believes in the time they invest in one weekly meeting.

Like all design teams, the group at Tyndale House attends plenty of meetings and are always scrambling for time. But every week, the group looks forward to a mandatory, two-hour-long meeting that seems to fly in the face of time management techniques.

Their design team meeting brings the entire department—about two dozen people—to a meeting which includes a business portion and a creative portion. The business segment is rather boilerplate, covering issues such as procedures, schedules, and the like. But the creative portion is where Senior Art Director Barry Smith says the real advantages of in-house design resides.

"We challenge one another's thinking, general design approach, and overall perspective on a project, and so are able to achieve a collective best. It gives us brainstorming opportunities, the showing of final design solutions, and everything in between," he says.

The regularly scheduled give-and-take necessitates thoughtfulness, both in what is said and how it is said. Watkins and Smith say this helps their team grow in their ability to respond strategically: when it's time to show their work to others outside of the department, their presentations are better. "We are accountable for our comments, which must be rooted in strategy and effectiveness, not loosely based on opinion," Smith explains.

The meeting's exact content has morphed over time, but two recent changes have made a big difference in its effectiveness. First, the team agreed that if they have strong concerns creatively or otherwise about a book making it to print, they must voice them here. If concerns are not discussed, they accept the blame for any problems that follow.

Second, whenever a designer makes a presentation of a book's design to the team, the new design is circulated to each team member with a template that has space provided for feedback and sketches. When the meeting is over, all of the sheets are handed back to the designer, who is then free to study and discuss specific feedback outside of the meeting.

"It has become core to our success as an in-house design team," Smith says. "You might be surprised by what a two-hour mandatory meeting can do to improve the overall creative product."

1 and **1** & **2** *(following pages)* As many people already know, a great way to be happy is to bring happiness into the lives of others. Tyndale House Publishers Senior Art Director Barry Smith and his staff make new authors who sign on with their company happy by sending an inspirational "author's book."
Designer and art director: Barry A. Smith; photographers: various

1

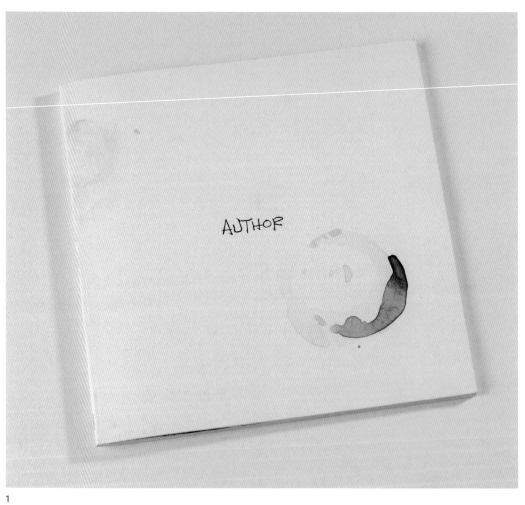

1

Tyndale House's two-hour, weekly, mandatory design meeting has specific guidelines for presenters and responders that help it succeed consistently.

Its goals:
- Build excellent design through collaboration
- Create team-building through affirmation and engagement
- Provide presentation experience for designers in a safe environment

Regarding newly finished products:
- Review the product's history and intended use
- The presenter/designer should highlight one or two elements of the design and acknowledge those who significantly helped along the way
- The responder should look for an element of the design to celebrate

Presenters of new or in-progress projects:
- State the nature of your presentation: already approved, in process, or brainstorming what you want from the discussion
- Give background to the project: synopsis, audience, purpose, author, format
- Give some personal identification with the project
- Mount comps and give print-outs whenever possible
- Be openly responsive and teachable. Admit when you are struggling with a design

Responders:
- Think before you talk; be relevant and concise
- Include positive feedback
- Keep criticism objective, never personal
- Practice giving feedback with language like, "This works because…" instead of "I like…" use "This is stronger because…" instead of, "I agree with…"
- Remember that our team includes other departments
- Everyone's opinion matters, regardless of role

Things to evaluate:
- The quality of the idea, its originality, and appropriateness
- Image content and style
- Type style, grammar, and hierarchy
- Use of color, contrast, and space
- Flow and unity
- Visualizing the spiritual dimension
- The presentation itself
- Pushing to the next level

Resource management

The in-house designer has many resources at the ready: manpower, hardware and software tools, creativity, business models, files, paradigms, and ideas. Selecting and managing the right resources plus an ever-pressing workload is a constant challenge. This requires that the designer has real insights into the organization's priorities and goals.

1

1 This Vita-Mix stand-up, flip-top recipe book was a 400-page project that required extensive revisions, says Elizabeth Schindelar, Manager of Creative Services for the company. "But with constant communications, we managed to produce it in about three months. A large project like this, with a looming deadline, requires the team to 'think as one.'"

"It is of utmost importance to build on the resources with the highest possible added value," notes Senk Aljosa, a designer and art director with the retailer Merkur in Slovenia. Added value is different for every organization, he says, and it is like energy in physics: it changes from one form into another and enables the organization to gain direct returns on capital.

People are the most valuable resource any in-house department can have. People with a wide range of skills are even more valuable. The New York Design Center, which is the name that has been adopted by the in-house group serving Harman International, a leading audio and visual equipment supplier, is divided into areas based on job functions: design, production, traffic, quality control/editorial, fulfillment, administration, and account service. "Many of our employees are skilled in two or three of these functions, enabling us to shift people where they are needed," explains Director

John Cianti. His department has been purposely built for the widest, deepest, and highest value.

Hiring people with broader skill sets increases the department's ability to be flexible and responsive. "We have copywriters on staff who also manage projects. Our web editor can also design and produce images for our website," says Diane Berno, Art Director for the Lance Armstrong Foundation. Even her own position gained advantage for the organization: she is a graphic designer with brand management experience, which enabled the foundation to take its communications projects away from a large branding agency and bring them back in-house.

David Lomeli, designer with sports entertainment company Upper Deck, works in a department where

"We aim to use our resources smarter, not be cheaper." *Diana Berno, Art Director, Lance Armstrong Foundation*

1

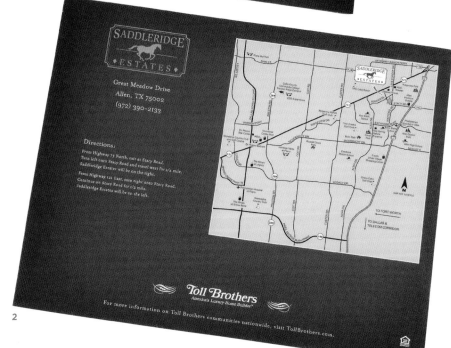

2

human resources are also organized for the best value. "We are a bit spoiled here because we have our own prepress department. We get to design and not worry about production. That helps us focus on being super creative," Lomeli says.

Other effective ideas for resource management include:

- Work closely with HR to solicit resumés for every position in your department, even those that are not presently open. in this way, your group can pre-locate ideal candidates before they are needed and fill vacant positions quickly.

- Plan ahead for how your department will handle absences, such as illnesses or maternity or paternity leave. Who is able to handle what duties or projects? How can the workload be spread out?

- Develop a good network of temps and freelancers who can help for short periods of time when needed. "You need to have that pool of resources ready," says Chuck Kijak, Manager of Creative Services for Crayola. "You need to establish relationships now so that you can go quickly to them later. You can be out there frequently looking for people." Mari Kaljuste, Art Director for Varrak, a publishing house in Estonia, stays in close

touch with a number of outside designers and artists to help design the 200 titles her company releases each year. "Sometimes we get together in the evenings for wine and to speak about our work. Every September, we have an autumn party, and I invite the outside designers with whom I have been in contact for the year to say thanks to them," she says.

- Develop a similar network with outside agencies for larger projects. "We don't send out projects that are core to our brand, preferring to only send out projects with a defined scope with defined parameters—think annual report versus collateral for an event," says Diane Berno, of the Lance Armstrong Foundation.

- Develop a solid brand style guide that anyone—new employees, temps, freelancers, outside agencies, the CEO of your company—can understand and use properly so that the work that is returned is on the mark.

- Effective management of visual resources is a must. The in-house design staff at TineMelk is developing an image bank and

1 & **2** and **1** *(following pages)* This design for a new community in Texas has unexpectedly saved designer Jason Gaghan a lot of time: management liked its design so much that it has become a template for brochures created for other Toll Brothers communities. *Art direction and design: Jason Gaghan; copywriter: Waleska Vega*

"You need people who will push quality and detail, and you need people who will pull for schedule and budget. If you don't have both, things will suffer."

Wendy Bogart, Director for Graphic Design for CASE (Council for Advancement and Support of Education)

A Note From Toll Brothers

At Toll Brothers, we build more than homes. We build *communities*. For 40 years, we've been building communities in picturesque settings where luxury meets convenience, and neighbors become lifelong friends. Toll Brothers is there — in the smallest finishing details of your home, in the setting that makes your home part of a neighborhood, and in the neighborhoods that create your community.

When you choose Toll Brothers, you are choosing our unwavering commitment to quality and customer service. We are honored to have won the three most coveted awards in the home building industry: *America's Best Builder*, National Builder of the Year, and the National Housing Quality Award.

But our greatest reward comes from the recognition we receive from our homeowners. As the nation's leading builder of luxury homes, we take pride in creating homes that are as beautiful to look at as they are comfortable to live in. Each Toll Brothers home offers a combination of quality materials and superior design, where every detail is meticulously crafted and every enhancement you select is seamlessly added to create a customized home that is uniquely yours.

Our commitment to excellence is reflected in the hundreds of distinctive Toll Brothers communities throughout the country and has earned us the praise and respect of thousands of homeowners — assurance that your new home will provide a lifelong source of pride and enjoyment.

The Toll Brothers Buyer Satisfaction Program

Our ultimate goal is for you to move into a home built to the highest standards. To make sure your home meets your expectations, we offer a unique two-step, pre-settlement orientation program. The first orientation takes place five to seven days before settlement, utilizing Toll Brothers' detailed checklist as a guide. Then, once again prior to settlement, you'll inspect your home to see that every item you noted at the first orientation has been addressed. The result is that you can entertain guests as soon as you move in! To give you lasting peace of mind, we also give you a ten-year limited warranty.

Toll Brothers Is Proud to Help Preserve Our Environment

At Toll Brothers, we believe that preserving the natural environment is an integral part of creating a community you'll be proud to call home. We take our commitment to environmental stewardship seriously.

Nationwide, Toll Brothers encourages environmental awareness and protection by partnering with conservation groups that include:
- The National Wildlife Federation
- The Audubon Society

Through these respected organizations, we've earned community certifications for programs such as Backyard Wildlife Habitats and Audubon Cooperative Sanctuaries for Golf Courses. These certifications assure our residents that the natural beauty of their communities will remain a proud legacy for generations to come.

The homes we build are specifically designed to harmonize with the scenic beauty of the surrounding landscape. We preserve as much open space as possible, incorporating the existing hills, trees, and ponds. As part of our award-winning conservation efforts, where possible we:
- Save and transplant thousands of existing trees
- Plant new trees throughout our communities
- Preserve and restore existing waterways
- Maintain designated open space
- Design communities that incorporate and conserve existing landscapes

Toll Brothers is the nation's premier builder of luxury homes and is currently building in Arizona, California, Colorado, Connecticut, Delaware, Florida, Illinois, Maryland, Massachusetts, Michigan, Minnesota, Nevada, New Jersey, New York, North Carolina, Pennsylvania, Rhode Island, South Carolina, Texas, Virginia, and West Virginia. With this experience behind us, you can be assured that your new home here in Saddleridge Estates will be a source of pride and satisfaction for many years to come. Toll Brothers, Inc. is the successor to three generations of home builders and is a publicly owned company whose stock is listed on the New York Stock Exchange (NYSE:TOL).

"It used to be that this office kept everything archived. Every time a client needed a new project, they would tell us about this logo we used two years ago somewhere—'Just use that.' To lessen the burden, avoid mistakes, and honestly, stop wasting so much time, we decided that the client's files would be kept for six months in our storage drive, plus two CDs of their files along with hard copies of their project would be archived. But they are now responsible for ownership of the project and keep their files for future reference. So far, so good."

Senior designer with a major medical and research center

media system that the whole company will be able to access when it is complete. The entire history of design for the company, as well as original imagery, adverts, brochures, campaigns, and more will be cataloged and entered into the master archives for ready retrieval.

Negotiation

Designers can be poor negotiators. The reason, though, is because they invest so much of themselves in their work. They also are often quite visionary when others can't or refuse to be. Situations are much more black and white—gray is a compromise that is just not acceptable.

That's not to say that designers can't learn to be good negotiators. There are plenty of books and websites out there that instruct just on that subject, but many of them focus on "winning." As an in-house

designer, though, you and your employer are on the same side: you need to create a true win-win situation when you present work, request resources, or attempt to reach some other settlement with people in your company.

The best way to think about negotiation is as a method of problem solving, not as a method of winning. One of the best tools for the in-house designer who is creating design work is a fully completed brief. It allows you to be very clear about what you want. On it, all of the parameters of the projects and priorities/wishes of the people involved should be listed in great detail. When the presentation is made, begin by saying something like, "We have addressed the brief in these ways. We agreed on this in the past, and I think you will see that we continue to agree on it." If your design truly meets the brief, it's much harder to beat down by argument.

All of the following are also crucial to the success of negotiation:

- Focus on the interests of everyone involved (including yourself), not on their positions. Try to understand each stakeholder's priorities. Get all of the parties together, if possible. Where people may not have opinions due to lack of information, provide the knowledge that they need.

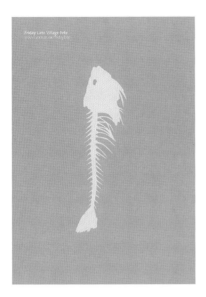

Friday Late Reflect
www.vam.ac.uk/fridaylate

❶ This series of postcards advertising "Friday Late" events at the Victoria & Albert Museum, had to be turned out quickly and inexpensively. The in-house (Contemporary Department) client who requested the cards was having a hard time finding appropriate images each month, so the museum's creative team came up with this bold, illustrative approach that is attractive to the target audience and is a fast, cheap print job.
V&A Design © V&A

Friday Late
Retro Bollywood
www.vam.ac.uk/fridaylate

Friday Late India Now
www.vam.ac.uk/fridaylate

1

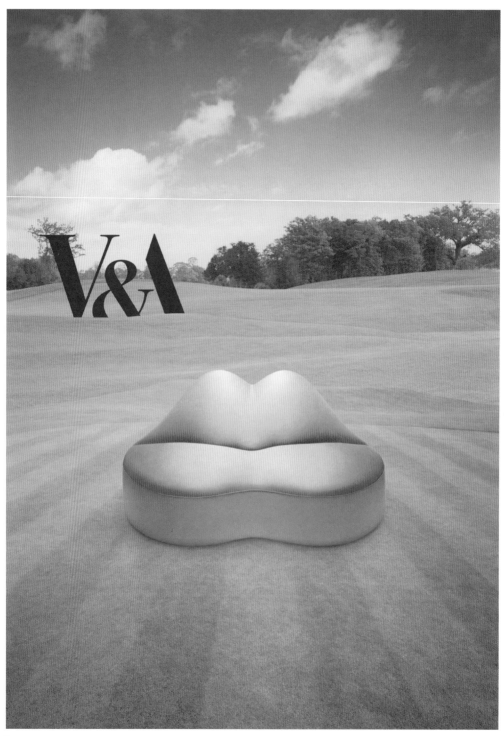

An invitation
from the V&A
and Crafts Council

2

1 The design explorations for the *Surreal Things* campaign were drawn out, says Victoria & Albert Museum head of design Jane Scherbaum. Dali's Mae West lips sofa was an obvious choice as the main image, but the designer had to work hard to convince all stakeholders that placing it in an unusual context would create a much more powerful statement. The design was a huge success: it was used across a wide range of print and media creations—including this invitation. "[The department store] Selfridges even recreated a version in one of their shop windows, and pink became the signature color for everything, from the lights in the museum's grand entrance to the color of the shop," reports Scherbaum.
V&A Design © V&A

2 For the *Out of the Ordinary* exhibition at the Victoria & Albert Museum, the designer of this invitation was keen to pursue a conceptual solution. But this approach was rejected, so a photograph of an existing work was sourced and then digitally enhanced. The results are beautiful, but, says head of design Jane Scherbaum, it was still a situation where not every battle can be won.
V&A Design © V&A

1

For instance, if you are presenting a new identity system, also show identity systems from allied groups with which they may already be familiar. Furnish information about new technologies or design trends to those who might normally not have access to them.

■ Know ahead of time what you are willing to sacrifice or change. Have a few legitimate options at the ready. "Always have a Plan B," advises one designer. "It's like a lawyer going into court: anticipate what they are going to say before they even say it. Sometimes, you will even have to present your Plan B first so that Plan A is not so shocking." Sometimes a short break is necessary to allow the designer to formulate an adjusted strategy. "Usually, I show more and various parallel ideas, but if these are not OK, I attend the meeting again the next day and try it another way," says Mauro Gazzaniga, an Italian in-house designer.

■ Decide beforehand what you will do if no agreement can be reached. Since you are usually negotiating about design-related issues, the next movement will normally have to be made by you. Perhaps you will have to go back to square one, which is not always the worst thing. "When we have really had to go back and rework something," says Jane Scherbaum of the Victoria & Albert Museum, "we always end up with something better."

■ Make sure everyone involved understands the process and feels involved. Often, people refuse to negotiate because they feel they are losing control and, therefore, respect or position. Listen to, respect, and most important, respond to those people's opinions, and they are likely to come back on board. Also, it's important for the entire group to sense and understand the benefit of the proposed agreement, and sometimes, this takes time. So be patient: until you can convince the group that what you are doing will benefit everyone involved, continue to follow up. Through persistence and evidence, you can build credibility. This highlights the fact that "negotiation" is often not a one-time event. Stick with it.

❶ There was some resistance to using an illustration instead of a photo on this poster advertising a fashion exhibition at the Victoria & Albert Museum. The designer, however, believed that working with the celebrated fashion illustrator David Downton created a unique look and feel for the campaign. The design was an enormous success: the exhibition attracted very high visitor numbers, and the image appeared all over London. It demonstrates the value of holding onto an original idea and going with one's creative instincts.
V&A Design © V&A

"At a past company, we were only allowed to use red and yellow because our president believed that those were the only colors other people took seriously. Everything had to be red and yellow. We lost, and he always won. And things always looked bad."

In-house designer with 10 years of experience, now with a new employer

1 & **2** and **1** *(following pages)* Outside agencies are a great resource, but only if the in-house group maintains very clear and positive communication from the start. The creative staff at Middlebury College created this extraordinary viewbook by allowing the design firm Philographica to bring a fresh perspective to the college.

Philographica Boston; photos: Bridget Besaw, Bob Handelman

Middlebury

what you'll find here
- a liberal arts education for the 21st century
- a community of diverse people and perspectives
- a passion for the environment
- a long-term commitment to international education
- people with the energy to make things happen

Portrait of a Study-Abroad Year

Rachel Rosenfeld '07, St. Louis, Missouri

Major: International Studies—Russian and East European Studies with religion concentration

Languages: English, Russian, Hebrew, Spanish

Viewpoint: During my year abroad, I gained not only an appreciation for other cultures, but also for my own U.S. culture. I learned about the interdependency between my communities here and my communities abroad, even though their relationship is filled with tension as well as support. I deepened my already existing passion to promote global awareness. Although religious and ethnic clashes divide us as a global people, there are nevertheless similarities to be discovered among various groups. As idealistic as it may sound, by emphasizing these similarities rather than differences, we can help unite people for a more peaceful future.

MIDDLEBURY RESOURCES Before studying abroad in the C. V. Starr-Middlebury Schools Abroad in Russia, Rachel spent a summer of intensive Russian language study at the Middlebury Language Schools. Her research while in Russia was funded by a research travel grant from the College's Rohatyn Center for International Affairs, and she drew on the center's unpublished source materials in her thesis.

FALL SEMESTER Rachel began her year abroad at Irkutsk State University in the southern Siberian city of Irkutsk, five time zones east of Moscow. She lived with a host family and was befriended by a local rabbi who helped her find interview subjects. Rachel also wrote a paper that was later published, and she served as the translator and narrator for an international film about the Irkutsk Jewish community.

54

RACHEL'S SENIOR THESIS *"Jewberia: The Struggle to Define Russian Jewish Identity in the Postmodern Period,"* an examination of the Russian Jewish identity crisis and its broader implications. *Adviser:* Assistant Professor of Religion and Classics Laura Lieber.

SPRING SEMESTER Rachel studied with Russian students at the Russian State University for the Humanities in Moscow and pursued a for-credit internship with Greenpeace Russia focused on global climate change. She lived with a host family.

udying for a semester in
and a semester in Moscow,
traveled through Russia along
ns-Siberian Railroad from
ow to Vladivostok conducting
ch for her senior thesis.

TRIP TO ISRAEL Before beginning the summer research, Rachel traveled to Israel, where she volunteered with students in the Russian Jewish community in Yokneam. She also interviewed Dr. Vladimir (Ze'ev) Khanin, a leading scholar of Russian Jewish identity and immigration at Bar-Ilan University.

LAKE BAIKAL While in Irkutsk, Rachel volunteered with two environmental organizations at Lake Baikal. This endangered body of water is the deepest lake in the world and contains 20 percent of the planet's fresh water. During a Middlebury-sponsored trip, she stayed in a traditional Russian banya on Lake Baikal and sampled smoked omul, a fish specific to the lake.

55

①-③ and ① *(following pages)* The *Self-described* book, a diversity brochure produced by the in-house design staff of Middlebury College, was 10 months in the making. But careful research and extensive interviews with students generated great stories, which guided the photography, which in turn drove the design.
Middlebury Communications Office

- Establish relationships with those involved in the negotiation before entering into the process. Also, make sure you have your "champion" or "angel" present: he or she or she may not be able to please everyone, but may have a weightier vote.

- Remember that the people involved in the negotiation (including yourself) are only that—people—and they all have different perceptions, emotions, and ways of communicating. Reactions may be personal and even hurtful: continue to listen, though, and try to stay above the fray. Stay professional, and don't take it personally. "Designers must have a thick skin," says Ella Rue, publications manager for New Jersey City University. "It's imperative that we use our creativity to somehow work out an acceptable arrangement for all parties involved."

- Know ahead of time what sort of conclusion is needed and communicate that to the other parties. Everyone involved must have the same expectation. For example, "Today we need to select the point-of-purchase designs that will be implemented in March." Perhaps absolute resolution is not needed on a particular day. Perhaps you only need the sign-off of one particular person in the room. Know what success looks like.

Self-described
Voices of the Middlebury community

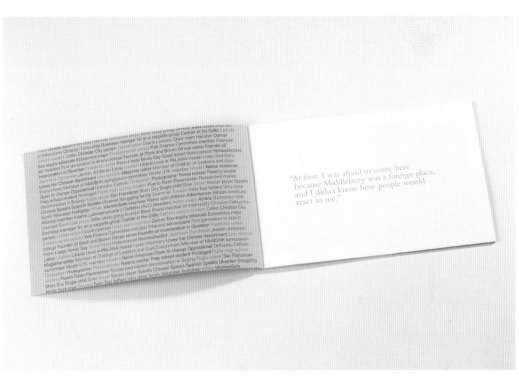

2

"At first, I was afraid to come here because Middlebury was a foreign place, and I didn't know how people would react to me."

3

Ethiopiah Al-Mahdi

MAJOR: ENGLISH AND AMERICAN LITERATURES
HOMETOWN: DORCHESTER, MASSACHUSETTS
FAVORITE: WATCHING THE SUN RISE OVER THE GREEN MOUNTAINS; READING ON BATTELL BEACH; CHATTING IT UP IN THE LIBRARY CAFÉ
ONE THING I AM: I LOVE WOMEN OF COLOR. WE ARE ALL BEAUTIFUL, AND IT IS TIME WE RECOGNIZE THAT AND EMBRACE IT

Now, I'm simply proud to be who I am.

Bryan Pacheco

MAJOR: SPANISH; TEACHER EDUCATION MINOR
HOMETOWN: NEW YORK, NEW YORK
FAVORITES: THE SMELL OF THE INDIAN RESTAURANT; THE MIST OVER THE FALLS FOOTBRIDGE
ONE THING I AM: A FILMMAKER

I come from Manhattan, the Lower East Side, and I am of Puerto Rican descent. I'm very close to my mother. She's always told me I would go to college. She dropped out of high school at 16, but then she went back and went on to get her master's degree. Because of her, I always knew I could succeed, no matter people's opinions or the obstacles.

I went to Catholic school with a majority of white students—I was one of the only Hispanics—and so growing up, when I wasn't in my neighborhood, I grew up thinking I was white. As soon as I came to Middlebury, I discovered that some people viewed me as a minority, which I had not seen myself as. Now, I'm simply proud to be who I am.

One thing I am most passionate about working with children. Middlebury h allowed me to tap into my activism to children. I choose my course load car so when I graduate, I can give back t Hispanic community, working with youth.

with shared experiences and open communication, a group develops into a safe

1 & **2** Sometimes the designer can save resources for the firm and the customer. In this case, Fidelity Investment designers combined four brochures full of confusing language and legalese into one book with much simpler instructions for the user. Creative Director Errick Nunnally says the resulting brochure has streamlined distribution for the company and increased understanding of the product for the customer.

Design: Errick Nunnally;
writer: Bob Heuska;
production: Jim Wheeler

1

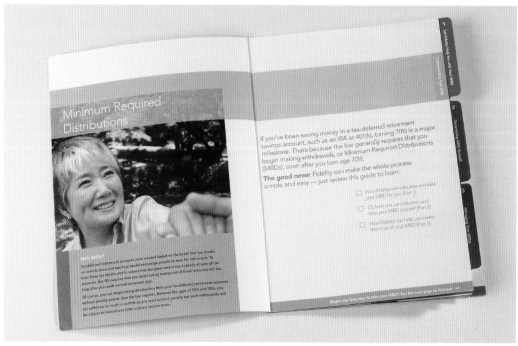

2

Setting benchmarks

From a purely practical standpoint, an in-house design department, although it may not generate hard revenue unless it's designing for-sale product, does save the larger organization money. It's simply more expedient for the organization to work with the in-house group—often they're in the same building which means less travel and hassle—and the group can often respond quicker and with no mark-up.

But that does not mean that the organization is always convinced of the group's value—and value equals respect. For the in-house group or designer who feels that respect is lacking, here are a number of techniques that have worked for others for setting scheduling and achievement benchmarks.

- "We have implemented a fairly successful tracking system that is akin to what many agencies use. We have job jackets for every project, and a FileMaker production schedule to keep track of 700-plus projects a year. Our e-system generates schedules that track dates ranging from 'first editorial review' to 'date due back.' Everything is filed in the jacket, and each week we have production meetings to stay on top of things. It's extremely helpful."

- "Set goals that are quantifiable. You don't want to say, 'Let's get jobs to press faster.' Instead, decide by how many days you can reduce the schedule. Then you can develop a strategic plan to make it real."

- "If I needed to, using software, I could do a financial analysis to prove an in-house person's worth compared to an out-of-house person. I can compare hourly rates versus low, medium, and high cost jobs. You need to be able to prove yourself by numbers. If you can get the respect of finance, you're home free."

- "The best way to get the attention of the client is to get the attention of the marketing person. It's always good to create an attention-getter, whether it gains positive or negative attention. If it's negative, it's a good learning situation."

- "Instead of just accepting the reactions of the remote company-owned sites that use our designs, I will try to find out

"There are some flaws in working for non-profits, but the best thing is how passionate everyone is. This is usually a good thing, but it also causes everyone to feel personal, often emotional, ownership over projects and to feel that their ideas are the best for the institution. This sometimes causes conflict between departments."

13-year in-house design veteran for a not-for-profit museum

"The perception is that in-house design is just overhead. I used to work at a company where I had a great relationship with the president. I remember how excited he was when he told me I was going to be moved from design to head up product development and new media. He said he was moving me from a profit drain to a profit center. I couldn't believe he didn't understand how valuable in-house design was."

Art director for an international accounting firm

what actually happened on-site. Maybe there was a problem on-site: there was poor customer service or no jobs came in that day. If we created materials for an open house, maybe they didn't conduct the open house at all, so the materials weren't even used. On the other side, I collect all of the positive comments as well, then pass the comments on to my managers. This creates an awareness of design's impact in our business. If we are doing great stuff and delivering it on time, then the outside offices aren't using it properly, that's when accounting or whomever gets involved and starts asking questions about why they aren't using what's provided."

"In any in-house design department, you are only as good as the value that is placed on you from higher up."

Mira Azarm, Assistant Director of Client Publications, University of Maryland

■ "I have started entering more contests. Our awards line the walls of our office. It makes us credible. Maybe we really do know what we're doing..."

■ "If a salesperson tells me that she used a sheet that we developed and it outlined everything perfectly for her customers, I make a note of that. Not everyone will give you that kind of feedback, but it's good to write it down when you do get good comments."

■ "On a daily basis, we meet each morning to set job priorities and set goals for the day. The heads of each team are there so that they hear it first-hand. Our client marketing people are also invited so they can advise us of any shifts in their priorities. They can also introduce new work at this time. I will also sometimes call the entire department together to discuss upcoming blocks of work and reiterate our priorities and responsibilities to each brand."

■ "Our standard for excellence lies not all in what we were able to design, but in how much more efficiently we could design it. Raising monthly quotas so that we produce more for our company is important to us. We have also begun to create concept pieces that help market our creativity and our ability to think outside of the box."

1

1 and **1** & **2** *(following pages)* For more than a decade, Korres (a producer of natural personal care and gift products in Greece) has worked closely with agency K2 Design to produce beautiful and innovative package designs and products.
Graphic design: K2 Design; photos of packaging: Stavros Papagiannis; structural design: Helene Prablanc

1

Case Study Rand McNally
Strategic Positioning

Joerg Metzner is Design Director for Rand McNally, the famous map company. He manages eight people, including a project manager, photo editor, design manager, three designers, production artist, and systems administrator. His group, which produces marketing and is involved in product development, has come a long way since he started there in 2004.

❶ & ❷ This packaging for a new cloth map product takes advantage of the nature of the soft fabric on which the maps are printed. "Rather than creating superfluous packaging that would talk about the benefits and characteristics of the product, we let the product speak for itself," explains Rand McNally Design Director Joerg Metzner. "All that was needed was a simple cardboard tent to label and hang the product. Sometimes less is truly more. Oh, and it did help with the budget."

"When I came here, this group was in a windowless room in the bowels of the building. It was called 'Art and Design'—no one knew where it was. I moved the department up into a large area with lots of light and no closed doors. There is a big table in the middle of our area. We changed the name of the group to 'Design,' and I gave a presentation to all of the managers of the company to introduce all of the changes. I told them we are not artists sitting around in berets waiting for inspiration. We are not here to make things pretty. We are here to help solve problems. We need to be involved early and strategically.

"One thing that is now crucial to our group is that we are the hub of the company. Everybody has to come to design sooner or later. I use that to really position us strategically.

"I know it used to not be clear what this group did. So we show lots of examples. 'This is how we can partner with you.' Also, we used to have a charge-back system, and when there were meetings, we would not get invited because everyone was afraid they would be charged for our time. So that system was thrown out. We really want to emphasize partnering.

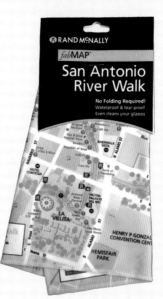

1

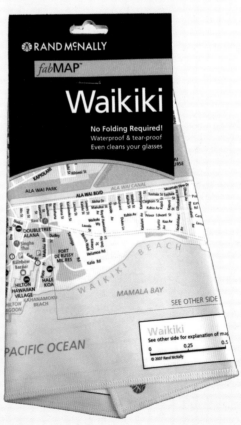

"Now we have time-tracking software that tracks customer time as well as task time—meeting time, design time, production time. When people come to us asking how long something will take, we can look back and tell them. Also, if we start to feel that we are stuck in meetings 80 percent of the time and we aren't getting to do our design work, I can put out a report that shows how much time was just spent fiddling."

2

① & **②** The first edition of this ride atlas was covered with Fibermark's Touché Cover stock, which has a unique, rubbery finish perfect for a motorcycle atlas—and much more cost-effective than using leather, explains Rand McNally Design Director Joerg Metzner. For a second edition, his staff used a synthetic stock, which made the cover waterproof, and printed a full-bleed photo. The changes between editions were cost-effective and clearly differentiated the two products.

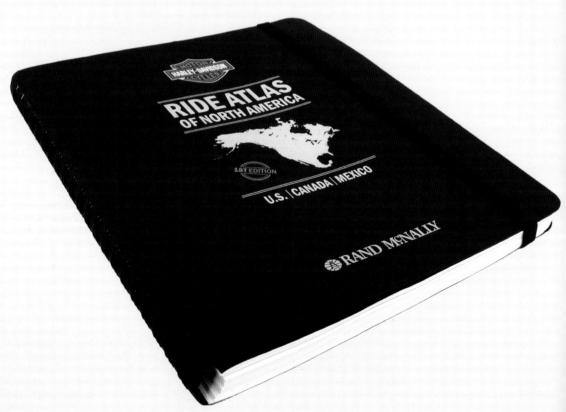

1

"We are the hub of the company"

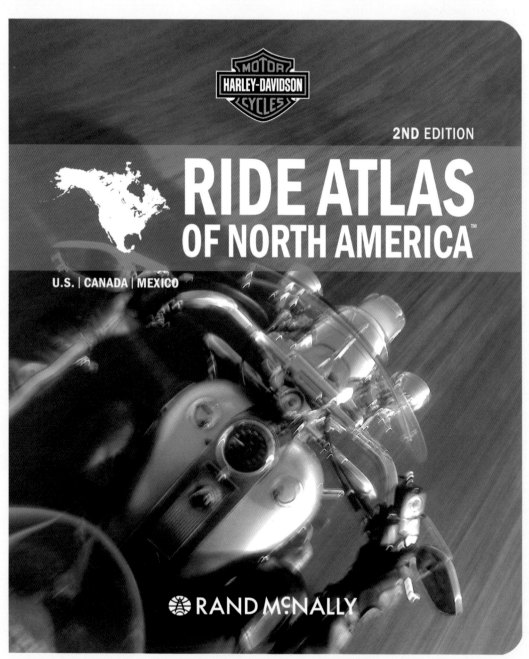

1

Fiddleproofing your designs

Design by committee? Everyone's-an-art-director-syndrome? Both are phrases the in-house designer knows all too well. Is it possible to protect your design while it's still within your control and police it once it leaves your reach? Yes, but it takes some amount of work.

- Get information up-front. One of the best ways to keep people from fiddling with your work is to not give them cause to do it. Know the target audience well; interpret the brand aptly for the assignment; and present clean, clear, and compelling work. Include an equally clear explanation of the design solution, and connect it firmly to the brief's initial goals (which you all agreed upon earlier).

- An educated client is always best. Teach everyone you work with about good design; train their eyes by sharing other successful work from outside of your organization. When others feel like they are an informed part of the process, and they recognize you as the expert, chances are, they will leave your work alone.

- Recognize different priorities. While you, as a designer, cringe at widows and orphans, those with whom you work probably don't even notice them. So when someone just adds a few more words to a carefully crafted block of text, creating a run-over that makes your skin crawl, remember that they do not have design training.

- Copywriters have different priorities than you. So does production, shipping, and nearly everyone else in your organization. A measure of compassion on the part of the designer is required, as is the ability to choose one's battles.

- Build a coalition. Keep the list of people who might be able to comment or approve/disapprove of your design very slim. Also, build a coalition of people who are likely to buy into your designs regularly and who understand the importance of your work. Once one of these people speak up on your behalf, it creates a domino effect that brings more and more people on board.

- Your coalition can also work well in reverse: if you send out an idea to them before you present it to the entire group, and that idea is summarily shot down, it's a good indicator that it probably isn't viable.

- Really listen. No matter how critical the comments, try to listen carefully to how people respond to your work. What are they trying to say, however strangely? Ask lots of questions. Why do they want green instead of red? Why do they want it to be pocket-sized rather than poster-sized? If you can address their concerns and even implement their ideas—even the tiniest ones—people will be less likely to give you grief later.

- Be a team-builder. Does your marketing material have persistent distribution problems? Are printing costs too high? Develop (and even become leader of) a group of like-minded employees who want to solve these ongoing headaches. It's much harder for people to pick apart designs or impose themselves into your work when you've created a sense of teamwork and fraternity in other areas.

- Find a strong leader. With a highly ranked vice president or other organizational leader in your corner, your work may have some added protection. But this is not a foolproof position: you do not have control over this person. On one day, he or she will fight for you; on the next, you'll be told to "let it go."

- Get a "brand officer." This is as close as you can come to having "brand police." An employee whose primary job function is to be the "brand officer" may be an extraordinary luxury for some organizations, but if you can prove the value to the larger

1 Sometimes it's best not to overthink what upper management is saying, says Elizabeth Schindelar, Manager of Creative Services for Vita-Mix. "When the sales director said to emphasize the advantages of using a Vita-Mix blender, the campaign was effortlessly born," she says.
Elizabeth Schindelar/Vita-Mix Creative Department

"Design by committee? It's not always a bad thing. You just have to choose who gets to be on the committee."

Art director with a large historical museum

group, it's absolutely invaluable. The design team's time is freed up to handle new work with the quiet confidence that enforcement is in place, protecting their work and preventing rogue design.

- Blind them with science. Use programs that they don't have and don't know how to use— InDesign, for example. Where PowerPoint Disease is rampant, look to newer options like Custom Show, which offers more design options and allows designers to administer changes to all versions of a certain file through master pages.

❶ & ❷ CASE, the Council for Advancement and Support of Education, offers its members hundreds of resources. But the organization also knows that simply sending out a complete resource guide once a year to busy professionals would mean that the guide's impact would be quite limited. So it supplements its ongoing message with smaller, quarterly guides as well as website contacts for every offering.
Integrated Marketing Department, Council for Advancement and Support of Education

- Master pages, in general, are a very handy tool. You can't completely forbid people from using unauthorized fonts or colors, but at least they will have guidelines.

- Establish a style guide. No matter how long it takes to compile, produce a standards manual that is accepted company policy. It will not only silently guard your work, but also educate others within your organization. (Try to remember that they don't use Zapf Chancery just to aggravate

you: they honestly don't know any better.) Work with your company's quality control team, if you have one: it will lend to the guide a better sense of "officialness." Include everything from proper color and font use to the grammar guides and dictionaries that your company ascribes to. Show samples of fonts, collateral designs, trademarked names, and as many other "what ifs" you can dream up. Get online and research the standards manuals of other companies for ideas on content and structure. No eventuality is too small or far-fetched to include. Let paranoia be your guide.

2007-2008

COUNCIL FOR ADVANCEMENT AND SUPPORT OF EDUCATION

The CASE
GUIDE
TO PROFESSIONAL DEVELOPMENT

A World of Opportunities

Fundraising
Alumni Relations
Communications and Marketing
Advancement Services
Advancement Management

November 2007–
February 2008

Germán O. Compos Valle
Director de Desarrollo Instruccional
Universidad Anáhuac
México

Director of Institutional Development
Anáhuac University
Mexico

1

2007-2008

COUNCIL FOR ADVANCEMENT AND SUPPORT OF EDUCATION®

The CASE
GUIDE
TO PROFESSIONAL DEVELOPMENT

A Year of Opportunities

Fundraising
Alumni Relations
Communications and Marketing
Advancement Services
Advancement Management

**THE COMPLETE RESOURCE FOR
ADVANCEMENT PROFESSIONALS**

Joanne Clark
Associate Vice Chancellor,
University/Community Relations
University of Hawaii
Honolulu, HI

think outside the guitar
continuous
worship

resurgence conference | also speaking: mars hill
featuring author: harold best |
pastors mark driscoll & tim smith
9.17-18 at the ballard campus | early registration:
$35 at theresurgence.com

redeeming female sexuality

Come learn about God's grace and glory, and the power of His redemption in all areas of female sexuality, including: sex within marriage, pornography, masturbation, promiscuity, same gender attraction, fantasy/romance novels, lust, and habitual sexual sin issues. Discussion and teaching led by women who are currently or previously struggling with these issues. **This teaching will not be recorded**. All Mars Hill women are welcome to attend.

July 14 | 1 to 6 pm | Ballard Campus

For women only — register at marshillchurch.org

2

❶ A smashed guitar is certainly not an image that most churches would consider using to advertise their programs. But designer Patrick Mahoney has, over time, included more and more conceptual messaging in his design, so that today, his overseers have come to appreciate his innovation.
Art director/designer: Patrick Mahoney; photographer: Greg Lutze

❷ Patrick Mahoney's daring design work for Mars Hill Church in Seattle has evolved over time. He continues to push the limits of his ideas with every project, and his superiors grow in their trust of his judgment.
Art director/designer: Patrick Mahoney

Case Study Texas Tech University
Underpromise And Overdeliver

Art director and designer Alexandra Dellis-Harcha discusses a project that was rife with challenges—small budget, short turnaround, bilingual, a large steering committee. Here, she describes how she directed the project in such a way that design could push forward to success.

❶ An assertive approach from the designer was essential for the successful completion of this complicated project. *Art direction, design, production: Alexandra Dellis-Harcha; copywriter: Cinda Courtney; client: TTUHSC Laura W. Bush Institute for Women's Health and National Speaking of Women's Health Foundation*

"This piece is copy/information heavy, bilingual, and very low-to-no budget. There was an executive committee in charge of the event. To avoid 'design-by-committee' (pun intended), I established at the start a timeline with deadlines for everything from art and photo submission to copy changes. I also had a 'contract,' which was a set of rules for the client—such things as 'no changes will be made by phone' and 'changes and approvals will be made by the designated person from the group.' It was signed by everyone and kept on the project file for future reference.

"For any project, have 'client deadlines' and your deadlines. Client deadlines are two weeks before the actual due date. This window allowed me to do changes without having to scramble at the last minute and having time to proof carefully.

"Another solution to the 'design-by-committee' challenge is to establish from the first meeting the go-to person in the group for changes and approvals; establish a limit on the number of changes; and let everyone know that the design process will not start until all the copy is finalized.

1

"Essentially, tough love was applied. Just because I'm an in-house designer, it doesn't mean my time is not valuable. The client must adhere to deadlines in the same way as if they were working with an outside agency. It doesn't mean you can't be flexible and accommodate the needs of your company. But you lose credibility if the department is not organized and doesn't have rules.

"Deliver what you promise, but always under-promise and deliver more and better than expected. That shows them that having rules helps you create great things, not just design that is 'good enough.' That shows that rules benefit them."

"For any project, have 'client deadlines' and your deadlines."

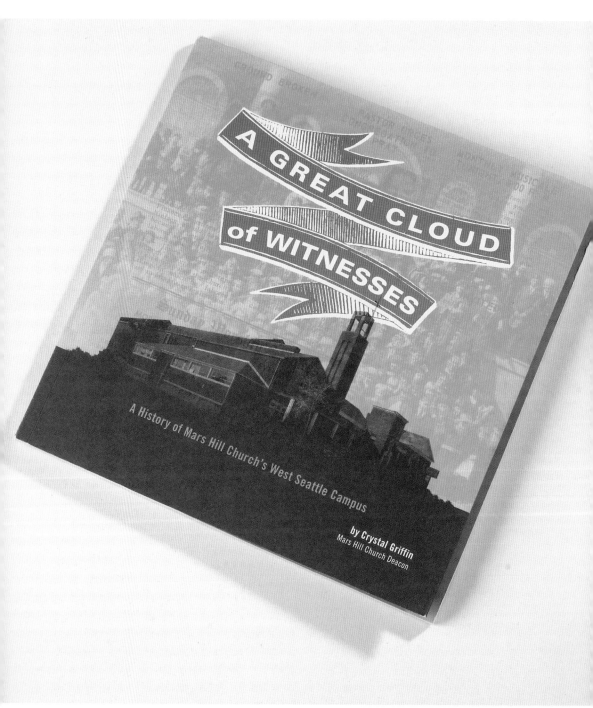

"We had designed a project that went through six rounds of changes, which was just insane. The biggest complaint we kept getting was, 'I don't like the font. It's not legible enough.' The font we were using was Arial—I don't know what could be more legible. Then the complaint was, 'I want a non-gender-specific font.' I'd never heard of that in my life. We really tried and went through a whole list of fonts for him, and in the end, he went right back to Arial."

In-house designer for an entertainment-based company

❶ & ❷ This small booklet, a history of Mars Hill Church, is unexpectedly modern in its design. Even old photos are portrayed in a contemporary way.
Art director/designer: Patrick Mahoney; printer: McCallum Print Group; author: Crystal Griffin

❶ The image of the crushed serpent that Patrick Mahoney had envisioned for a card advertising his church's Good Friday service was already strong. But he also went to his superiors with a request for a big, bold, blind emboss. "It would be somewhat expensive, but it was Good Friday, so it reflected the impressiveness of the day," he says. He got the go ahead.

Art director/designer: Patrick Mahoney; printer: McCallum Print Group

3

In-House Design in Context

Working Your Way Up

Jenn could not have been more excited: she and her fellow designers had been entering design competitions for several years, and they had scored several local successes. But this time they had hit the jackpot: several pieces of the in-house team's work for the company was going to be featured in an international design magazine. The group had already planned a night out to celebrate.

Jenn had wasted no time in sending the good news on to HR, who liked to send out company-wide emails on special achievements like this. The notice about her department had just hit her inbox.

"Please join us in congratulating the graphic design team for a very special recognition. Their work for our 2007 annual report, collateral system, and new logo design will be featured in a publication that focuses on graphical design."

"Graphical design?! What? I give up!" Jenn's production manager appeared at her door, shaking a copy of the curiously worded e-mail.

"It's OK," said Jenn, smiling. "They understand that we scored big—that's all that matters."

Gaining feedback and freedom

With feedback or freedom, be careful what you ask for: you might just get it.

"You need to establish yourself as the expert, but you can't be so tied up in your expertise that you don't listen anymore. If someone is saying that something isn't working for them, you have to find out why." *In-house designer for a large science museum*

The right kind of feedback can be great: reaffirming, inspiring, energizing. So can more creative freedom. But too much or the wrong sort can be almost paralyzing.

The right kind of feedback

Everyone loves a compliment. But feedback can be hurtful, too. A manager may be being truthful when he says, "I just don't like that," but the response is as meaningless as it is uncaring. A vice president might come bustling in with a sketchpad full of her ideas for the website you've been slaving over night and day for weeks: what sort of feedback is that? The knee-jerk response is, "Butt out."

Because people are much more prone to complain than they are to compliment, most of us learn to dread the word "feedback." It has a negative connotation, though, that it really doesn't deserve. As most leadership and business methods training will tell you, feedback is a gift, whether it's good or bad. Another person is trying to reach out and communicate something to you. If you are truly concerned with the ongoing success of your employer, it's incumbent on you to listen.

If you can stop considering feedback as something bad that is inflicted on you, you can begin to gain value from all such communications. Start to distinguish between varieties of feedback: are you getting a compliment, a comment, or a complaint?

"Ask for feedback by a specific date. Let them know ahead of time that if you do not hear back from them by that date, you will assume that you can go on to the next step. If they do not reply on time, they can't complain later."

Elizabeth Schindeler, Senior Designer, Vita-Mix

- A compliment is self-evident: "I love the new website." Sometimes, though, it can be of the backhanded variety. "This website is so much better than the one you guys did last year!" can be hard to swallow. Ignore the ingraciousness, extract the compliment from the snarl, and savor it: the person is trying to be nice, however awkwardly.

- A comment is simply neutral: it's usually an observation and nothing more. But it can sometimes sound like a complaint, if you let it drift in that direction. It's easy to start reading too much into comments like, "Look's like you're finally making progress on that brochure." What does that mean? It means that the other person has noticed that you are making progress on the brochure. Nothing more.

- A complaint, however discomforting, can be very useful to you. Let's go back to the old favorite: "I don't like it." What can you do with that?

TINE ER HOVEDSAMARBEIDSPARTNER FOR HUNDREÅRSMARKERINGEN

En hundreårsmarkering kan gjøre noen og enhver av oss litt nostalgiske

TINE har vært på norske bord i generasjoner. Hva var vel da mer naturlig enn å hente frem noen gode minner i forbindelse med Hundreårsmarkeringen. Husker du blomsterdesignet som prydet melk-, fløte og rømmeemballasjen på 70- og 80-tallet? Husker du varme vafler med brunost og kald melk, eller kjempestore bursdagskaker med jordbær og masse krem?

1

1 & 2 TineMelk
designer Kristin Olsson
was cleaning out office
files when she found a
portfolio that contained
TineMelk package designs
from the past. The images
struck a nostalgic chord
in her, and with the help
of an outside firm, her
team resurrected the
theme in a contemporary
way. The feedback she
has received from
TineMelk customers,
she says, has been
entirely positive.
Dinamo Design, Kristin Olsson,
and Andrew Moen of Tine BA

2

① Further examples of the TineMelk packaging. The patterns and colors help customers to differentiate between the various milk grades available in the range.
Dinamo Design, Kristin Olsson, and Andrew Moen of Tine BA

1

Transform negative to positive

- When this sort of feedback arrives at the wrong time—say, when you're on deadline for another project, or when it is a surprise ambush, delivered in the middle of an unrelated meeting—quickly regain control of the situation. Ask the other person if you could talk about this later, when you can better focus on the concern.

- It's up to you to translate what exactly that person is trying to say. What exactly does he not like? The color? The typeface? The entire concept behind the project? Clarify what the person is saying by restating his words: "You don't like it because of what specifically?" Stay calm, don't get defensive, and thank the other person for their input.

- Listen, listen, listen. Use the kind of body language that tells the other person that you are hearing what they are saying. This does not mean that you have to put their every word into action. It does give that person a sense of validation, however, and that goes a long way toward resolving conflict. If necessary, take notes.

- Ask the other person what he thinks should happen next. "OK, now that I understand your concerns better, what should we do next?" Stress "we" as opposed to "I." Keep the problem-solving process one of teamwork.

Once you have received the feedback at an appropriate time, in words you understand, and know exactly what the other person wants, you can respond. It may be a matter of offering some sort of design education or history on the project: "There's a lot of white space on the cover because it draws the customer's eye in quickly," or "We had to use that blue because the job is going to be ganged with our stationery on press in order to save money."

Getting any feedback at all

Sometimes it seems as though you're working in a vacuum. After an enormous push to deadline, a job gets done on time and on budget, and you see it on its merry way. And you hear... nothing. No accolades, no complaints, no nothing. What then?

"When no one complains, but no one says 'great!' either, I follow up. Sometimes you have to draw people out," says Jessica Merete, a designer with Pitney Bowes. "Also, when people stop by and say 'awesome!' and I ask them, "Why do you say that?' they usually look at me like I have two heads. These are not creative people, and they just don't articulate in that way."

If someone is simply unable to verbalize what she wants to say, ask if that person can bring in samples of other design work that she does like. Use that material as a point of departure for an insightful discussion rather than beating your own work to death: it puts both people involved in the discussion in a much more neutral space.

If soliciting verbal feedback seems too awkward or unproductive, consider developing a printed or emailable form that can gather feedback for you. Solicit answers that you can actually use: "What did you like or dislike about the photos in this piece?" instead of "Did you like the photos in this piece?" Yes or no answers are not useful.

Sometimes feedback comes in, but not in a timely manner where it would be useful. Fikile Gotami, an in-house designer in Zimbabwe, struggles with geography: many of the people from whom he wants feedback are in far-flung locations. So he tries to get feedback early in the design process and respond to that. "Any response helps make our products take a better direction and construction becomes easier and more comprehensive," he says.

Finally, to prevent "style wars" or "grammar battles," have your company-approved standards guide and dictionary and style

---

"When there is a person who is being hurtful [with feedback], we try to take it with a grain of salt. I may sit down with the designer privately and mentor them on not getting discouraged. I tell them that they have a right to be upset, but that we need to show them who the real professionals are. I may also just try to offer a better perspective—for example, say 'Maybe this is what the person is trying to say.'"

Joerg Metzner, Design Director at Rand McNally, on coaching designers

through negative feedback

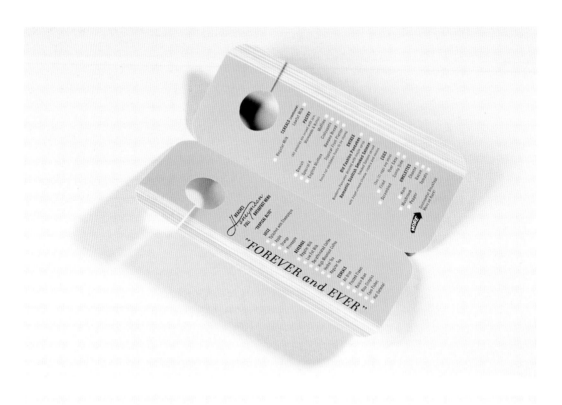

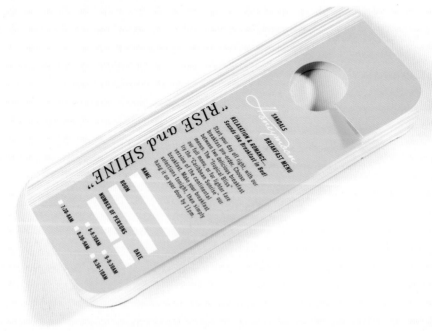

❶ & ❷ Unique Vacations' Senior Designer Scott Peiffer knows he is on track when guests at Sandals and Beaches resorts (represented by Unique) take home the designs he creates. The smaller door hanger (shown left), he says, is the number one appropriated item.
Senior designer on Property Media: Scott Peiffer

guides at the ready. Certain things are simply not up for discussion, and standards that are already deemed as "official" by the organization are among them.

Getting more creative freedom

Lack of feedback may sometimes seem like the endowment of more creative freedom—after all, if no one's complaining, doesn't that mean that everything's going swimmingly? Not necessarily. Lack of feedback can signal apathy, that others are too busy to respond, or someone is out on vacation.

There are a number of ways to earn more creative freedom. The following are simple techniques that have worked for other designers:

- Start by asking for it. The answer might be surprising and gratifying. Or, look for windows of opportunity, no matter how tiny. For instance, volunteer to take on a new creative challenge that is outside of your normal duties.

- Work larger, higher, and deeper inside of the project parameters. A brochure will be printed on paper, but what kind of paper? Push for something completely new and different. The catalog needs product shots—but do they have to be the same as they have always been? Shake things up a bit.

- Push the boundaries out a little at a time. Scott Peiffer is an in-house designer for what would seem to be a very conservative client—a large church in Seattle. But the design work he produces is exciting and challenging. He often has very few resources—no copywriter, no art, and very little time. But over time, he has gained the trust of his supervisors by being resourceful and responsive. He has consistently done good work, so they trust him to do more good work in the future. "Once I did a poster [relating to female sexuality] which gave my overseer some concerns. He liked it, but he was still concerned. We negotiated: I told him I would show it to five women, and if none of them had any qualms, we could go with it. I did, and they didn't. So we went with it, and I think there was one negative reaction from the entire church," Peiffer says. "There is more acceptance of challenging work over time. Each job I do pushes it a little further."

- Fikile Gotami recommends careful planning in the early stages of a project so he can build in time for some self-awarded creative freedom time later.

"Creative freedom comes when the client falls in love with the designer's ability to say, draw, and develop what the client cannot."

Tyler Moore, an in-house designer with Accretia

1

■ Display your ability to be strategic. Mira Azarm, Assistant Director of Client Publications at the University of Maryland, recalls a situation where she suggested that the four different enrollment guides her admissions office produced each year be put on CD. She also recommended that all of the different forms incoming students needed be placed on the school's website. "It's scary to think about big changes like this, especially since I'm essentially taking work away from our department," she says. "But doing these things made it easier for the people using the materials, and with the admissions office budget freed up from these four pieces, we could have more fun with other pieces. It comes down to being open-minded: that's how you get more freedom. Think of a better way to do things, and people will let you do it. Whenever people are looking for a different way to do things, there is an opportunity for the designer to produce real change."

● This packaging gave the design team at Advance Auto Parts more creative freedom than usual due to its nostalgic flair. The unique packaging also won several ADDY awards.
Senior designer: Marcie Phoebus; creative director: Shawn Murray; production designer: Danny So; printer/ manufacturer: Li & Fung

①–③ The entire creative culture of a company can be driven by its in-house designers. These remarkable "bubble shoes" were designed by Aljosa Senk of the Merkur Group, a major home and industrial products supplier based in Slovenia, well-known for its history of innovation. This design turns the concept of what a shoe is upside-down: The sock worn inside dictates the fashion the wearer wishes to display. *Idea, concept, and design: Aljosa Senk; renderer: Goran Jamicic; client: Armada d.o.o.*

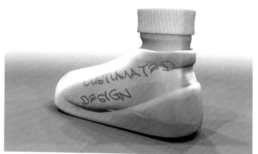

2

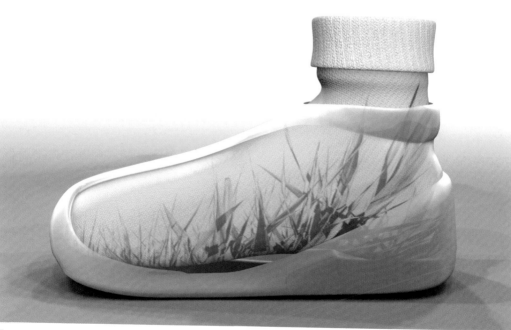

3

Case Study   Andy Epstein
Entrepreneurial Spirit

At the time of this interview, Andy Epstein was in transition, moving from a director position at Bristol-Lyers Squibb to a consulting assignment at Johnson & Johnson. Epstein has 20 years of in-house experience and is the founder, with Glenn John Arnowitz, of InSource, an association of creative professionals dedicated to providing support to the in-house community.

"It's the underlying challenge that all in-house designers face: how can you be entrepreneurial inside of a corporation? Can you shoehorn an entrepreneurial model into a bureaucratic environment? Where can you get the corporation to bend, and where can you carve out as much space for your team as possible?

"You walk in at a disadvantage. Directors of marketing and communications have assumptions about how [outside] agencies are creative, and in-house groups are just there to crank out the work. You have to be very proactive in battling those assumptions. For example, if you get an assignment that is not particularly creative, you can offer more options, options that are over and above what they wanted, just to strut your stuff.

"I remember an instance when we had a then-rare opportunity—at the very last minute, because the agency was falling flat—to come up with advertising themes. But they told us not to mess with the logo— the agency had already handled that. Of course, in addition to doing the ad work, we did some new

> **"Directors of marketing and communications have assumptions about how agencies are creative, and in-house groups are just there to crank out the work."**

1 BMS had been using a generic black-and-white photo approach for adverts for more than five years when it asked its in-house team to update the look. Creative director Andy Epstein and his team chose color- and image-rich illustrations to communicate a much wider range of corporate attributes.
Creative director, Andy Epstein; illustrator, Scott Dustman; designer, Tim Lee

1

logos as well and just slipped them into the boards that held the ad treatments. They liked the designs and asked us to work them up more. Eventually, out of the six logo designs that were focus grouped, four were from the in-house group, and the final choice was also ours.

"We took the initiative, and as a result, we got more creative work. We earned a tremendous amount of respect. After that, we also created vehicles that showcased our work inside the company—CDs, leave-behinds, email blasts. When allowed, we also entered competitions. It was amazing how much respect that would garner when we won.

"We also had the accounting firm Ernst & Young do an audit for us and quantify the cost savings we brought the company. The group took 100 projects and compared the cost to that of doing the work out of house. We discovered we were saving 70 to 85 cents on the dollar. We validated our value by going to an outside group who already had credibility with upper management.

"What I discovered is that it is very possible to be entrepreneurial within the larger corporation. We worked with upper management and used business-approved models to make our arguments to gain more respect, more freedom, and enhance our value."

Celebrating your successes

Number of designers interviewed for this book who readily admit that they do nothing to celebrate their offices' successes? Roughly eight out of every 10, surprisingly enough. Likely, this low figure is more attributable to the ongoing crush of work that most in-house designers face than it is to any self-appreciation deficit. But it's a missed opportunity: sharing good news is a very effective tool for gaining respect within the organization and for building a sense of confidence and teamwork within the department.

"Affirmation is crucial," says Senk Aljosa, a designer with the retailer Merkur. "Affirmation that comes from outside is usually stronger than that generated within a company. It facilitates ambition and functions as an elixir, improving the employees' ecosystem."

Consider these simple methods:

- If you or your department have undergone recent training or won any awards, send out an email to let everyone know. Think of it as a way to market the in-house group and advertise your growing expertise and abilities.

- Don't limit yourself to sending in work to competitions sponsored by design associations or magazines. Talk to your printer about entering printing awards shows. There are also associations galore out there that are specific to your organization's work (higher education, for instance, or entertainment) who also host their own letterhead contests, website competitions, and more. Even local business associations and chambers of commerce host events that can yield gratifying recognition for all of your hard work.

- When you win awards, take the time to frame and hang them or find prominent shelf space on which to display them. If you can get duplicate plaques or certificates for the clients who were involved, order them so they can celebrate with you.

- Offer yourself up as a speaker for outside organizations. For instance, business clubs are always looking for lunchtime presentations: talk about building a successful identity program or (even better) why having an in-house design group makes so much sense.

- Here's a way to stretch your creative muscles and promote your good work: publish a small newsletter, e-zine, or other periodic publication that does

"Part of a good reward system is being able to talk openly about stuff, to be able to blow off steam when necessary in a safe environment."

Joerg Metzner, Art Director, Rand McNally

the bragging for you and distribute it internally. Let the design of the piece also demonstrate the kind of design you are normally not called upon to do.

- When a project is finished, write up a case study, using your work as illustrations. Post it in the cafeteria or other common area. Emphasize the teamwork throughout, crediting not only the designers but also those outside of the department who contributed to the success of the piece.

- Offer your team what rewards you can, even if it's a bit under the radar. If it's possible for a team member to work from home for a morning, make it happen. If it's possible to use budget money for restaurant certificates or training courses, figure it out. The reward does not have to be great, just sincere.

- Organize a research day and take your entire team to an art exhibition, on a long hike through the woods, or to a large library. If you can swing it, take everyone to a cool restaurant and spend the time brainstorming and getting to know each other.

- Get team members to the training events and professional conferences they request, whenever possible.

"At one time, if someone did something exceptional for the company, he or she would get a monetary reward. When the company started having some financial troubles, they offered free lunch coupons to the company cafeteria instead. It was a Band-Aid approach that was so cheap that it was insulting."

Long-time in-house art director with a large personal care product manufacturer

- Rotate workload, especially if you have projects which repeat regularly—like an annual catalog, for instance. One designer might be more experienced in pulling it together, but perhaps a great reward for her would be to pass it off to someone else so she can try something new.

- Create a microsite onto which you can post all of your department's work. Its purpose is to be promotional/informational and attract new recruits. When fellow designers see their work presented as examples of good design that is solid enough to represent the company to potential new employees, it gives them motivation.

- Be a little surreptitious. "During one particularly busy time," confided one art director, "I had a masseuse come in and give massages to everyone. Sometimes it's better to ask for forgiveness than permission."

- Be a little subversive. One designer working for a very large corporation tells the story of how

Case Study **Selfridges**
A Creative Culture

Ashleigh Vinall is Head of Graphics for Selfridges, the well-known British retailer. It is a company that truly values and embraces design, using it as a tool that sets it apart. Vinall explains here how she and her small team of six people are able to produce such a varied and powerful range of designs, usually on a very short time schedule.

"Selfridges is a creatively led company. It values creativity. There's a respect here for graphics and designers. It comes from the top down. When you walk around the store, you see it.

"Our Creative Director is on the executive board, which can be quite unusual for a retail company. But it helps creativity to filter down throughout the culture of the company. The ultimate decision about graphic issues is with the Creative Director, the Marketing Director, and myself.

"When I'm trying to convince people, I always show them rather than tell them."

"The company can be run this way because everyone is very clear on how we do things. I have worked elsewhere where there are a lot of people commenting on the design work. It's the famous scenario where the buying team who are purchasing shirts and such tell you they want blue on the brochure. But I don't comment on the shirts they are buying—I don't have that knowledge. I don't know the minutia of buying. This doesn't happen here.

"That does not mean that the feelings of internal clients are not heard and valued. If someone says they don't like something, I have a tick list in my mind to find out

1

exactly what they don't like. The color? Paper? Type? Maybe they don't like blue, but it's because they had an awful blue bedroom when they were a child!

"Often I have people asking to make the message bigger so it shouts better. I have a simple visual way to prove my point. I have a piece of paper that is just crammed with sales messages and information, and I have another sheet that simply says in very small type '20 percent off' in the center. I ask them, 'Which one would you read? Which one will our customers read?'

"When I'm trying to convince people, I always show them rather than tell them. Visuals are always so much more persuasive."

❶ A culmination of a two year review/ assessment of instore point-of-sale ticketing, these new templates have been designed to be on the one hand flexible enough to carry a variety of information, while on the other being rigid in terms of typographic styling. *Art direction, Ashleigh Vinall; designer Ashleigh Vinall*

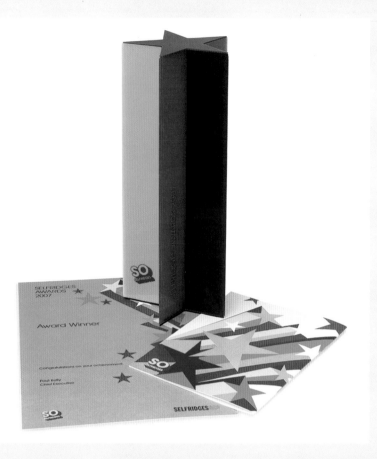

1

1 Identity created for the Selfridges Internal Awards, which celebrate the achievements of the company's staff. The design had to be flexible, bold, and exciting, expressing the glamour and glitz of an award ceremony. *Art direction, Ashleigh Vinall; designer Lee Curtis*

2 This invitation and CD were part of an extensive range of collateral that the in-house team creates annually for Christmas. The brief was to create an identity that was contemporary, clean, and expressed the essence of the season. *Art director, Ashleigh Vinall; designer, Jessica Wells*

2

3

❸ Three from a set of nine characters created for the instore promotion of Mother's Day, designed by Selfridges' in-house designer Lee Curtis. They depict many different personalities of a "Mom" being fun, fashionable, and colorful. The characters were used across a wealth of instore collateral from posters, banners, and tickets to photo frames and much more.
Art director, Ashleigh Vinall; designer/illustrator, Lee Curtis

❹ Here are just a few examples of an extensive range of designs created for The Selfridges Selection of own-label food. All designs had to clearly portray the individual characteristics of the different products, as well as sitting together as a complete range. The designers were involved in creating not only the surface graphics, but also the stucture of the packaging.
Art director, Ashleigh Vinall; designers, Jessica Wells, Lee Curtis

4

1

2

3

❶ To reflect the freedom and expression of the Punk era, Selfridges designer Jessica Wells created a strong, edgy typographic style and identity which was adopted across all print for this large in-store promotion. Shown here are examples of an invitation to the launch party, plus posters used to advertise the event inside and outside the store. *Art director, Ashleigh Vinall; designer, Jessica Wells*

❷ & ❸ "Working with a huge variety of brands, these seasonal brochures highlight the breadth of beauty products available in Selfridges. We maintain creative control over all photography, layout, and print, ensuring the brochures not only promote the breadth of product but also the integrity and quality of Selfridges as a brand," explains Ashleigh Vinall. *Art director, Ashleigh Vinall; designer, Jessica Wells*

"There is certainly some kind of stigma attached to in-house design. But I think being so closely tied to the client allows you to have a truly entrepreneurial spirit."

Joerg Metzner, Design Director, Rand McNally

his company issued a three-page memo on how to use the new turnstiles by the front entrance. His group countered with an instructional pamphlet on how to use the bathroom. "People have to feel safe enough to laugh and have fun," he says. "The company gives you so much ammunition. And I think that a little subversion builds teamwork. Fear is what destroys the collaborative, creative process."

Remaining inspired

Whether you work inside of a large corporation or for the tiniest of not-for-profits, it can be very difficult to remain inspired as a designer. In the first situation, ridiculous corporate-inspired paranoia and processes are often rampant, staggering into your path at every turn. For the latter, resources can be scarce and you may be working alone.

A sense of under-appreciation and isolation can emerge. How can you find validation? How do you fight boredom when you are always working on the same brands with the same people?

"One of the most depressing things to see is someone who has lost the ability or the willingness to fight

and who always wants to go with the safest option," says Jane Scherbaum of the Victoria & Albert Museum. "You need to unlock something in that person. Why are they struggling? Perhaps I can give them something different to do for a while. Sometimes I might suggest they work in a different environment—at home for the morning, maybe. Perhaps if we can acknowledge his successes more, he will get that pride back."

- Try something different. You may feel locked in by your employer's marketing messages or product lines or identity. But there are no rules that say you can't mess with that stuff unofficially, on your free time. "Take the brand in different directions, even for an hour or so a week" encourages Everett Keyser, a designer for a casino. "How would it look if it was applied differently? Then when the brand does change, you might already have a good body of work to show management."

- Get involved. Become involved with professional design associations. Volunteer for causes who could really use and will likely appreciate your design talents.

- Become a teacher. Communicating your skills to other people can be extremely validating. Offer to teach at a junior college or community center, or offer to give select classes at a school. Assist professors or mentor students involved in a design program at a local university or college.

- Become a student. Promise yourself that you will take at least one outside class or seminar per year. You might perfect some computer skills or learn to throw pots. What's important is to be a life-long learner.

- Read, read, read. Read everything. Subscribe to magazines, check out books, scour museums. Don't just stick with design. All new information brings with it the opportunity for new insights. Don't forget blogs and websites.

- Moonlight. "Most corporations won't like this answer," says one long-time in-house designer who asked not to be identified, "but the one thing I have done that has brought me the most creativity and perspective on my in-house work—and kept me from burning out—is freelancing. It is a huge help. It gives me a break— different topics, different clients— and it's just plain fun." There's another benefit, he adds. "The perception of the designer in the freelance equation is that you are more valued. You are in a different seat."

"Toys from Archee McPhee. I will also clear the air with the person I'm most discouraged with."
University art director on staying inspired

- Create your own website. Many in-house designers have their own websites, where they can display their personal work and show the world an entirely different side of their being.

- Upgrade and uplift. Ask the organization if you can upgrade hardware or software: equipment is something the company does understand, and some larger organizations have entire purchasing departments in place to help you do it. This can provide a long-lasting boost throughout the department. "Switching to flat screens for us was just huge," reported one creative director.

- Change your space. The single most mentioned way to improve one's sense of creativity and fun is to create a workspace in which it is a pleasure to be every day. There are a number of different tacks that can be pursued.

- Can you actually put some physical separation between you and the maddening crowd? At Crayola, the in-house design

"I did once work for a magazine in a large city where we were on the 18th floor of a building that overlooked downtown. I had a floor-to-ceiling window. It was still a miserable place to work."
Museum designer

1

team is located in an old mill building, about 10 minutes away from the corporate headquarters. If it's impossible to be actually sequestered, at least decorate in a way that clearly communicates that this is a very different space, unlike the rest of the organization.

- Alternately, maybe your in-house department would be better placed at the physical center of the organization, its role as a symbolic hub represented by its actual place.

- When you must live in cubicle world, make those walls as low as possible. What is lost in privacy is more than made up for in collaboration and a greater sense of space.

- Hang up your work so that others in the company can see it. Spread out magazines. Hang swatches of cloth, or art samples, or anything that inspires you. Create a sense of experimentation and fun that makes others want to visit you.

- Shape a space that creates focus. Fred Machura, of the advertising and graphics department of the shoe manufacturer Skechers, says that their space is almost like a bunker or a lounge. "It is a centralized, closed-off area where the walls are faux cement with no windows. Custom lighting is kept dim, and we have backlit bookshelves for reference materials. At the center is a large light table where the team can meet and build comps," he says. "The result is a room that really keeps us focused. A big plus is that we work in Manhattan Beach, in California, one block away from the beach. Being that close to the fresh air and openness is a huge plus."

1 & **2** The workspace for the advertising and graphics department of Skechers is almost like a bunker, isolating and focusing designers on their creativity.

2

Case Study Museum of Science, Boston
Making A Fresh Start

Fanny Lau is an Art Director and Designer for the Museum of Science in Boston. Her group found a unique way to celebrate their successes and create an exemplary workspace at the same time.

1

❶ The design team's office at the Museum of Science: before (left) and after (right).

❷ The team created "brand" T-shirts to celebrate their new initiative.

"This is my favorite team achievement. With the launch of our new branding initiative, we took the opportunity to overhaul our physical office as well, so that other departments could recognize our 'fresh start.' We did extensive space planning, maximizing our current footprint, gutted the office, got brand-new furniture, paint, and accessories.

"Then we held a company-wide open house and portfolio show where we made 'brand' T-shirts, had a decorate-your-own-branded-cupcake competition—in brand-colored frosting, of course—showed PowerPoint mini-bios of each team member's monitor as a get-to-know-us device, and more."

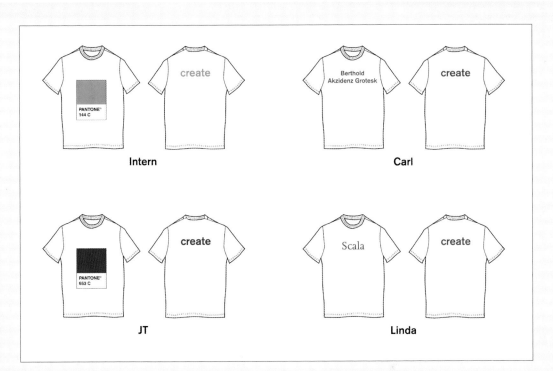

Intern

Carl

JT

Linda

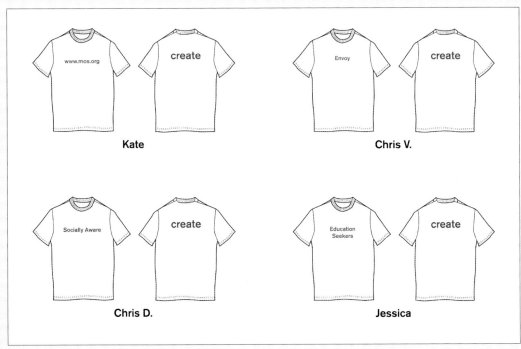

Kate

Chris V.

Chris D.

Jessica

Case Study **Room & Board**
Designing Creative Space

Jill Brynes of Room & Board, a furniture and home furnishings company, is an in-house designer in a unique position. Since she works for a furniture manufacturer, she not only has become knowledgeable about the subject of exemplary workspaces, she also works in one.

❶ & ❷ The designers at Room & Board enjoy the best of both worlds: an open, collaborative work space, and a quiet, private area for meetings and detailed work.
Photographer: Adam Torres / Room & Board

"Last year we did a restructure. Everyone knows that your power in the office has a lot to do with where you sit—boss in the corner office, right? Today I sit with my team, and I'm not in an office anymore. The designers are on the perimeter of the area.

"We used to have walls between teams. Now we have literally cut holes in those walls. The new open workspace has developed a sense of shared ownership in all of the projects. People are less territorial.

"But even though collaborative space is great, sometimes you do need quiet. For that we have an area with sofas and a workstation where you can go for private conversations or estimating or whatever else you need to do in your own head.

"Access to natural light is critical to people's mental health. We have a courtyard right outside of our area that affords plenty of natural light, but we have shades to limit it if necessary. For other lighting, you need halogen overhead lights, natural occasional lights, and task lights. Task lighting especially counteracts the blue cast of fluorescent lighting. It is warmer and helps define spaces.

1

"For work surfaces, take advantage of different levels. Sometimes people want to stand and talk, and sometimes they want to sit and gather. Create different sorts of gathering areas: we have a large, long conference table as well as a small, round conference table. We tailor the space to the types of meetings we have.

"The more open and collaborative the space, the more your team will become like that. It's up to the creative leaders to provide this sort of space. Stake out your territory within the company."

2

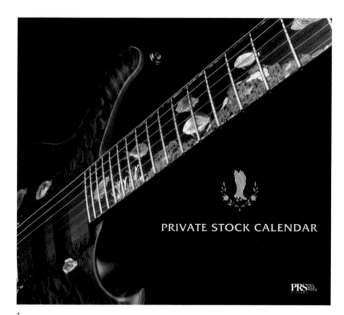

1

1 & **2** Many designers would be envious of the products that designer Alexis Somers gets to create materials for: beautiful, intricate, colorful guitars. All of these samples are from her portfolio. She stretches her skills and gets re-inspired by working on completely unrelated projects together with fellow designers on a design-related online discussion group.
Art direction: Marc Quigley; design: Alexis Somers, Marc Quigley; photography: Jim Noble, Marc Quigley, James Derdock, Alexis Somers

Developing new skill sets

Growing new skills on the job can prove difficult as there are always deadlines or projects that require a designer's attention. Finding and taking the time necessary to learn anything new or develop an existing skill set can be challenging, but it's crucial that designers do so. New skills are new tools that help the organization now and the designer over time.

The familiar training standbys are seminars, conferences, books, magazines, newsletters, CDs, and DVDs. But there are a number of other methods that also work well.

- Keep an open mind. Try to remain as open as possible to new experiences. Kevin Longo, who works in marketing for the magazine *Entertainment Weekly*, is being encouraged to develop more and more competencies in interactive design, although his first love is print. "It really helps so much. It makes you reexamine your priorities and recognize that the whole world is not print," he says.

- Build a wish list. Even when you can't attend training conferences and seminars, study the offerings on their mailings carefully. What subject matters are being stressed? What new areas are being explored? Such simple considerations can help you keep your department's wish list current.

- Explore alternate resources. Alexis Somers of PRS Guitars recommends Lynda.com. "This wonderful resource, good for visual learners like me, offers video clips on a wide range of subjects and software programs. The clips are not terribly long, which makes it possible for me to squeeze one in here and there," Somers says.

- Practice, practice, practice. Somers also advocates practice as a learning skill. She does this not only through her work for PRS, but also by working with a group of other designers on the HOW magazine discussion board: together, they created a themed, handmade book that really had

2

nothing to do with their normal jobs. "That project allowed me to stretch my mind and to practice skills that might be new or aren't currently being utilized at work," she says.

- Mentor someone. A comfortable mentoring relationship provides a safe place in which to exchange skills—and the mentoree can offer as much as the mentor, particularly if that person is much younger and has the latest computer skills.

"I had all of my people take a class on written communications. If you send something to a client with misspellings and poor grammar, you lose credibility. Or, you might not be selling well, or are just wasting time by being too wordy. Some staff members were very passive-aggressive about the course. But some have really embraced it and have moved beyond where they used to be. With any kind of training, you have to show the other person that you are concerned with their best interests, not just wasting their time."

Long-time art director who works with an international drug and personal products corporation

2

1 & **2** Designer Scott Peiffer of Unique Vacations (the worldwide representatives of Sandals and Beaches Resorts) uses what might be considered challenges to push his creativity. For this project, he needed to steer guests to specific activities on a particular property. To save on time and resources, he sketched by hand, retraced fonts, used the copy machine, and employed other "handmade" techniques. Two of the resulting designs are shown.

Senior designer on property media: Scott Peiffer

1 With no budget and an advert to design, Alexandra Dellis-Harcha, a resourceful Senior Designer in the Communications and Marketing department of Texas Tech University Health Sciences Center at Amarillo, collected her digital camera, some simple props, a big white sheet, and Photoshop. The result was fast and cheap, but fun and attention-grabbing.

Art direction, design, production, copywriting: Alexandra Dellis-Harcha

■ Hire the right skills. As TineMelk of Norway has developed its in-house design department, it has been careful to create a combination of people with different skills—illustration and design, packaging design, web-based design, marketing, and experience in working with outside design firms. Each of these people is able to share their skills with the others.

■ Share the wealth. If your department doesn't have enough budget to send everyone to a conference, just send one person with the understanding that she should be prepared to teach everyone else once she returns. One in-house department enforces this passing on of information by making it an actual check-off entry in the annual review process: to receive the highest review scores, each person must pass his or her training on to others.

■ Learn from external designers. Designers with outside agencies sometimes have different competencies than those who work in-house. So it can help to pick their brains when you have

access. How do they present to their clients? What software configurations are they using?

■ Getting involved with professional design associations can be invaluable. Most offer local conferences and get-togethers where you can garner new skills and stay current on design issues.

■ Think strategically. If you think that you might be able to save the company a lot of money by handling, for example, tabletop photography, in-house, build a case that could earn you a training course in photography plus some equipment. Show the organization through real numbers how the investment makes good business sense.

■ Develop business savvy, too. Don't neglect the development of your business and leadership skills as well. Management skills make an in-house designer highly marketable, both within the organization and when they decide to move on. Other areas for possible improvement include public speaking, purchasing, writing skills, dealing with difficult people, and estimating.

■ Work with vendors. Paper suppliers, printers, hardware providers, and more may be more than willing to offer specialized and free training to your group right on site. Just ask.

"Most designers don't think of university design groups as cutting edge. They think things like, 'Oh, you have to use the school colors on everything—how exciting is that?' We have to show people what we really do and the range of what we do."

Experienced in-house designer with a large North American university

SUMMER'S HERE.

Enjoy your summer family time in good health. Visit us!

We provide a wide range of medical services to care for
you and your family's health needs.

Texas Tech Physicians
of AMARILLO

1400 Coulter • Amarillo, Texas | For appointments call 354.5600

1

"I've worked at both agency settings and in-house. I'm the perfect client for any agency because I know their problems. And I'm their worst nightmare because I know their problems."

Creative services manager for a large restaurant supplier

What lies ahead?

One of the greatest powers any designer possesses is the ability to be a visionary. Where will my company be in another year? Where will I be in another year? Will I be able to improve my circumstances? The exact answers may not be clear, but the vision of what could be is always there, lurking and hopeful.

One thing is certain: change is coming. And if you agree with chaos theory, it's easier to deal with the resulting tectonics when that motion is in the butterfly stage rather than the F5 tornado finale. Be ready. Be watching for it to begin.

It's difficult for one individual designer to have much effect on the entire forward motion of an organization, especially a large one. The best advice is that which has been offered throughout this book: continue to be an effective leader through your design and communication abilities, and you will be part of the organization's success.

Also pay attention to the corporate landscape as it relates to in-house design: change is already afoot. More organizations are bringing in

1

2

1-**4** Since 1992, Illy Café has sponsored the Illy Art Collection, sets of espresso cups and saucers decorated by artists of all media. The company's in-house creatives continue to develop the now-famous cups: 66 collections and more than 70 artists now help connect the Illy brand to the pleasures of enjoying coffee and art.
1: Dream, by Shizuka Yokomizo; 2: Spirali, by Roberta Pietrobelli; 3: Daniel Buren; 4: Italian Riviera, by James Rosenquist

3

4

❶ & ❷ A great way to develop new skills is to work with an outside company. POLI.design, a part of Politecnico di Milano which works to tie university study directly to industry, created everything from the package design to store displays for a new line of spa care products. Projects such as these constantly place new experiences in front of the POLI.design team.
Design: POLI.design, Luisa Collina, Andrea Mansiaracina

contract employees, even for managerial roles, to save on costs and risk. Creative staffing agencies such as Aquent are playing a larger role in staffing, too. Production work is being out-sourced overseas.

Your rights

You need to know your rights as they relate to building a portfolio. Every situation is different, but in general, as a full-time employee, your employer holds the rights to all the work you create. This is especially pertinent if you are creating logo and identity work, because those lines of design are almost always work-for-hire arrangements even for outside design firms.

Does this mean you can't show any of the work you created as an in-house designer in a portfolio? Not necessarily. The best advice is to ask about the company's policy on fair use in advance, right when you are hired (or even while you are interviewing). If the practice is acceptable, start saving work immediately (PDFs may create the most consistent record-keeping, as some companies won't consistently provide printed samples). If it is not, you may need to consult an intellectual properties lawyer to get a better handle on what you can do in your particular situation.

If approval was not gained at the outset, it's wise to ask for permission now. In a recent legal

1-**3** This project, carried out by POLI. design, part of the Politecnico di Milano, represents an attempt to develop an exclusive line of clothing and accessories for an academic institute. "The intrinsic technological quality of this facility led us to develop its image to specific chromatic and material variables that reflect the mood of its campus," explains Art Director Umberto Tolino.

Design: Umberto Tolino, Luisa Collina, Chiara Columbi, Alberto Sala

1

2

case, an artist who created some work but who did not hold the rights was fined $150,000 after she used it in a portfolio.

There are other options:

- Show work that you have created as a freelancer or as a volunteer for other organizations.
- Describe in words what you did for the company. Provide a website address to the interviewer where he can look at the work.
- Provide plenty of references who will speak on behalf of your work.

Other ways to think forward:

- Keep your resumé up to date, even if it's just a job title or duty description update.
- Know how to design for web and print.
- Know the latest programs, and be able to work on PC and Mac.

"What I love about working in-house as compared to an agency is that we are automatically sought out for creative decisions and don't have the high agency price tag. We're the go-to place for anything creative—product design, producing a training video in a Scandinavian country, changing a price in a catalog, helping with a fund-raiser, or helping to decide what color to paint the building."

Elizabeth Schindelar, Vita-Mix

- Keep a professional outlook, even in your clothing: remember that you are operating in a corporate environment and need to look professional.
- Keep your resumé in the files of recruitment agencies. Let friends, contacts, and suppliers know that you may be looking for a new position.
- Know what you're looking for. Do you wish you had more vacation time? More flexible time? Better benefits or money? Have your wish list ready.

① & **②** It's very difficult to accommodate all of the needs of a large organization, such as a university, in an identity. It's even tougher to know what needs the organization will have in the future. The design team at POLI.design, part of the Politecnico di Milano, created this identity, which easily accommodates new imagery and entities while creating a very consistent look. Note how both posters use the same grid yet have a very different look.

Design: POLI.design

Resources

Professional organizations

AIGA
www.aiga.org

American Marketing Association
www.marketingpower.com

Aquent
www.aquent.com

Art Directors Club
www.adcglobal.org

D&AD
www.dandad.org

Design Council
www.designcouncil.org.uk

Design Management Institute
www.dmi.org

InSource
www.in-source.org

International Council of Graphic Design Associations (ICOGRADA)
www.icograda.org

Competitions/shows

Art Directors Club Awards
www.adcglobal.org/awards

CASE
www.case.org/Container.cfm?containerID=127&navID=0&crumb=2

Clio Awards
www.clioawards.com

D&AD Awards
www.dandad.org/awards

GD:USA In-House Design Competition
www.gdusa.com/contests/aida.php

HOW magazine InHOWse Design Awards
www.howdesign.com/competitions/IHDC_51468_ad1.pdf

Red Dot Design Awards
www.red-dot.de

Conferences

InHOWse
www.inhowseconference.com

International Design Management Conference
www.dmi.org/dmi/html/conference/overview_s.htm

Mind Your Own Business (MYOB)
www.howbusinessconference.com

Publications which support in-house issues

Dynamic Graphics
www.dynamicgraphics.com

HOW
www.howdesign.com

Communication Arts
www.commarts.com

Graphic Design:USA
www.gdusa.com

Blogs and online forums

Design Observer
www.designobserver.com

Graphic Design Forum
www.graphicdesignforum.com

HOW blogs
www.howdesign.com/blogs

Software of special interest to in-house designers

Traffic (project management)
www.sohnar.com

Basecamp (remote collaboration)
www.basecamphq.com

Index

Thanks

So many thanks go to the brave and resilient in-house designers who were willing to share their insights and enthusiasm about in-house design, a field that is equally full of opportunities and land mines. Their sharing spirit, wit, and camaraderie have shown the way for many others. Special thanks should also be given to Glenn John Arnowitz, co-founder with Andy Epstein (who also generously contributed to this book) of InSource, the first independent support organization expressly for in-house designers, for providing early feedback and the great foreword; to the editorial staff of *HOW* magazine, which actively addresses the business interests and human concerns of in-house design; to the tremendous staff at RotoVision for championing the under-addressed field of in-house design and giving me so much fantastic guidance; to my ever-patient sons for putting up with so much take-out food and still loving design and drawing; and to Denny, the human safety net, who steadfastly monitors the Rant-o-meter through every project and serves up a hard lemonade and an easy smile whenever conditions seem to warrant.